MEDITERRANEAN COOKING

EDITED BY Joseph F Ryan, PhD and Jillian Stewart
DESIGNED BY Philip Clucas, MSIAD
FOOD PHOTOGRAPHY BY Jean-Paul Paireault and Peter Barry

5122 Mediterranean Cooking
This edition published in 1999 by
Bramley Books

ISBN 1-84100-126-0
Printed at Oriental Press, Dubai, U.A.E.

MEDITERRANEAN COOKING

Bramley Books

Contents

INTRODUCTION

*There is a special, almost indefinable quality
to living in the Mediterranean region.*

Clustered around the shores of the Mediterranean, ancient Arab, Greek and Roman philosophers, in the course of rarefied debate, sought in vain to define the essence of the 'good life', perhaps because the answers to such mysteries are often too commonplace to be recognised for what they are.

Where philosophy fails, art can sometimes provide an insight. Under the dazzling Mediterranean sun, successive artists have transformed their work into expressive swirls of luminous colour. But the brilliant light they chose to praise is not entirely responsible for the health and contentment of the peoples of the Mediterranean.

Happily, the solution to this conundrum is available to everyone, for surely it is the food and wines of the region that so admirably nourish and sustain the inhabitants, while it is the sun that brings the harvest to ripeness.

THE SPICE OF LIFE

Traditional wisdom has always suggested a balanced diet as a sound foundation for a healthy lifestyle. To achieve this balance and to maintain enjoyment, nutritional variety – the

real spice of life – is of major importance.

Fortunately, the cultures that encircle the Mediterranean are very diverse, and the diet ranges from the fragrant foods of North Africa, to the delectable meals of the Middle East and the sophisticated cuisine of France, Spain and Italy. Ingredients include vegetables such as artichokes, aubergines, broad beans, okra, courgettes, fennel, mushrooms, onions, radicchios, spinach, sweet peppers and tomatoes. Besides rice, grains encompass couscous and cracked, or bulgur, wheat. There are also the pulses, a wide number of dairy products, fruit, pasta, nuts, herbs, spices, flavourings, oils and, straight from the sea, Mediterranean prawns and a range of appetising fish.

From this cornucopia of food, it is possible to make a wide range of mouthwatering meals. Fresh, natural ingredients are brought together to create an attractive blend of colours, textures and tastes. The Mediterranean diet, therefore, is distinguished by its variety, flexibility and flavour. It is also highly evocative of the region, conjuring up azure skies and warm seas, the glare from golden sands, the brilliant hues and exotic aromas of the marketplace, and landscapes that shimmer in the heat.

A HEALTHY DIET

The delicious spectrum of foods available, however, is not just of advantage to those with a discerning palate. Current research suggests that the traditional Mediterranean diet may be responsible for a low incidence of medical disorders such as heart disease, high blood pressure and stroke, as well as some digestive ailments and forms of cancer. Now it is possible to eat good food as an intrinsic part of an enjoyable and fulfiling lifestyle without endless worry about harmful consequences.

The Mediterranean diet comprises a mix of foods that is exceptional among Western industrialised countries whose peoples typically have a soft, sweet, very refined, additive-loaded pattern of consumption that is also high in animal fat. In particular, the normal Western diet includes an excess of saturated fats, which are found in meat and dairy products, and are known to raise blood cholesterol levels. Raised cholesterol is highly implicated in all forms of disease resulting from obstructed blood flow, such as heart attacks and strokes. This is because it causes narrowing of the arteries and forms into clots, thereby blocking the blood supply to the brain or heart. It is convenient, therefore, that both garlic and poly-unsaturated fats can contribute to lowering cholesterol levels as these are often used in Mediterranean recipes.

MAGICAL OLIVE OIL

There is another remarkable feature of the Mediterranean diet. It has been noted that people in some of the poorer areas of the Mediterranean, like southern Italy or Greece, consume a

diet fairly high in monounsaturated fats, yet have a death rate from coronary heart disease that is half that found in the United Kingdom or the United States. It has now emerged that the important factor in this is the use of olive oil, which is widely used in the typical Mediterranean diet.

Olive oil is believed to offer protection in other areas, too. The most easily digested of fats, it has been shown to be effective against stomach ulcers. Perhaps most interestingly, however, its regular consumption may be a protective factor against the ageing process. So, olive oil may also be an elixir of life, keeping people fit and healthy for longer!

NECTAR OF THE GODS

The Mediterranean diet has a further secret preventative in its repertoire: wine! Across the millennia, the wisdom of the Bible has instructed: 'Drink no longer water, but use a little wine for thy stomach's sake and thine often infirmities'. The sun-soaked vineyards of Mediterranean lands provide the finest grapes, and the people are happy to indulge. Medical opinion has finally joined this consensus, admitting that a little red wine each day seems to offer some benefit by reducing the clot-forming tendencies within the body.

The recipes in this book have been chosen from all around the Mediterranean and are both easy to follow and delicious. Each meal captures within it an authentic taste of the sun, and transports the gourmet to a world of relaxed living that is still maintained wherever the warm waters of the Mediterranean lap the shore. So, prepare one of the meals, relax, and allow yourself to be transported to a land of sensory delight.

Soups and Starters

There can be few better ways to gain a first taste of Mediterranean cuisine than to sample some of the delicious soups and starters featured in this chapter. Recipes range from a healthy Greek feta cheese salad for a summer's day to a heart-warming Algerian soup for a cold winter's evening. But there are many other tasty dishes, such as Sprats in Mayonnaise, Stuffed Eggs, a delicately flavoured mousse and aromatic Bean Soup with Saffron. These light dishes delight the palate without cloying the senses, and leave the diner eager for the next exciting course.

Above: **Rolling dough in Turkey.**
Left: **Martigues in Provence, France, is a colourful resort frequently visited by artists wishing to benefit from the Mediterranean light.**

MINESTRONE

Contrary to what one might think, hot minestrone soup is delightful served as a starter on a hot summer day.

INGREDIENTS

SOUP:

115 g/4 oz broad beans, pre-soaked overnight

2 tbsp olive oil

115 g/4 oz piece of bacon

1 carrot

½ courgette

2 medium-sized potatoes, peeled

55 g/2 oz peas (shelled, fresh or frozen)

115 g/4 oz pasta shells

SAUCE:

10 fresh basil leaves

2 tbsp pine nuts

1 egg yolk

1 clove garlic, finely chopped

175 ml/6 fl oz olive oil

Salt and pepper

30 g/1 oz finely grated cheese (Cheddar or Parmesan)

SERVES: 2-4

1 Rinse and drain the beans. Heat the 2 tbsp olive oil in a saucepan and sauté the beans and the bacon for 1 minute.

2 Pour over plenty of water and cook for 45 minutes, or until the beans are cooked.

3 Cut the carrot, courgette and potatoes into small pieces. Keep the potatoes in water and set the other vegetables aside.

4 To make the sauce, crush together the basil leaves and the pine nuts. Add the egg yolk and garlic. Gradually whisk in the olive oil until the sauce thickens like mayonnaise. Season with salt and pepper, add the grated cheese, stir well and set aside.

5 Add the carrot, potatoes and peas to the beans and cook for another 15 minutes.

6 After 15 minutes, add the courgette and pasta and cook for a further 15 minutes.

7 Remove the piece of bacon; chop and serve it, accompanied by the sauce, for guests to garnish their soup.

Time: Preparation takes about 35 minutes, plus overnight soaking. Cooking takes 1 hour and 15 minutes.

CHICKEN SOUP WITH VERMICELLI

Home-made chicken soup is always delicious. Serve this Algerian recipe as a starter for a winter meal.

INGREDIENTS

2 tbsp butter

1 carrot, finely sliced

1 bay leaf

1 onion, finely sliced

1.15 kg/2½ lb chicken carcass (bones and meat), broken into pieces and flesh roughly chopped

½ leek (white part only), finely sliced

Salt and pepper

55 g/2 oz vermicelli

2 tbsp chopped chives

SERVES: 4

TIME: Preparation takes 30 minutes and cooking takes 1 hour.

1 Heat the butter and gently fry the carrot and bay leaf for 2 minutes. Add the onion and continue cooking for 2 minutes. Add the chicken carcass and meat and fry, shaking the pan, for a few minutes.

2 Pour over enough water to cover the ingredients. Stir in the leek and season with salt and pepper.

3 Cook on a moderate heat for 45 minutes, adding extra water if necessary.

4 Strain the contents of the pan through a fine sieve, reserving only the stock.

5 Pour the stock into a clean saucepan, bring to the boil and add the vermicelli. Cook for approximately 2 minutes and serve sprinkled with the chopped chives.

Freezer tip: The stock can be frozen at the end of step 4. Defrost and reheat gently. Bring to the boil, add the vermicelli and continue as for step 5.

Cook's tip: If the stock is a little too fatty at the end of step 4, place it in the refrigerator for 30 minutes, then skim off the layer of fat which has risen to the surface and continue with step 5.

Variation: Try other vegetables in the soup; the choice is wide and entirely up to you.

KORIATIKI SALAD

This feta cheese salad from Greece is flavoured with a variety of fresh herbs.

INGREDIENTS

4 tomatoes

½ cucumber

1 onion

115 g/4 oz feta cheese

1 tbsp wine vinegar

A little oregano

3 tbsp olive oil

Salt and pepper

1 tbsp finely chopped olives

1 tsp finely chopped mint

1 tsp chopped chives

SERVES: 4

TIME: Preparation takes about 20 minutes.

1 Cut the tomatoes, cucumber and onion into thin, even-sized slices.

2 Prepare a piece of feta cheese (or other crumbly sheep's cheese) by breaking it into small pieces.

3 Make a sauce by beating together the vinegar, oregano, olive oil, salt and pepper.

4 Delicately mix together the tomatoes, cucumber, onion, feta cheese and olives. Season with the sauce and sprinkle over the fresh herbs before serving.

Cook's tip: If you are not using fresh feta, do not crumble it, but cut it into small cubes.

Serving idea: Vary the sauce by substituting lemon or lime juice for the vinegar. Serve in a small bowl for guests to help themselves.

Above: The Parthenon, chief temple of Athena, on the hill of the Acropolis at Athens, Greece.

ANDALUSIAN GAZPACHO

A rich and tasty cold soup, full of the summer goodness of its native Spain.

INGREDIENTS

6 tomatoes

1 cucumber, peeled

1 green pepper, seeded and pith removed

1 red pepper, seeded and pith removed

1 stick celery, cut into 4

½ small chilli, seeded and roughly chopped

1 onion

2 cloves garlic

2 tbsp wine vinegar

Salt and pepper

115 ml/4 fl oz olive oil

GARNISH:

2 slices smoked ham, cut into small cubes

8 black olives, finely chopped

¼ yellow pepper, seeded and cut into small cubes

1 tbsp olive oil

4 slices bread, cubed

1 Cut the tomato, cucumber, peppers and celery into small pieces and place in a blender with the chilli, onion, garlic and vinegar. Blend until quite smooth. It may be necessary to blend in batches.

2 Force the mixture through a sieve to eliminate any pips.

3 Season the gazpacho with salt and pepper, and beat in the olive oil. Chill the soup for 2 hours.

4 Just before serving, fry the cubes of bread in 1 tbsp olive oil until golden.

5 Serve the soup accompanied by the croutons, smoked ham, olives and yellow pepper.

Freezer tip: This gazpacho can be frozen before the olive oil has been added. Defrost, blend smooth and then beat in the olive oil and serve with a little extra sprinkled on top.

Cook's tip: Be careful when preparing the chilli – wear rubber gloves or wash your hands thoroughly after handling it.

SERVES: 4

TIME: Preparation takes about 30 minutes, plus 2 hours chilling.

PEARL BARLEY SOUP

INGREDIENTS

55-90 g/2-3 oz pearl barley, soaked overnight

1.8 litres/3 pints chicken stock

Salt and pepper

175 g/6 oz bacon, diced

1 tbsp chopped parsley

220 ml/8 fl oz natural yogurt

1 egg, beaten

Juice of 1 lemon

1 tbsp chopped chives

1 Drain the barley and rinse in clean water. Add to the stock along with the seasoning, bacon and parsley. Cook for about 1½ hours on a low heat.

2 Beat the yogurt into the egg and add the lemon juice in drops, beating thoroughly.

3 Remove the soup from the heat when the barley is cooked and briskly beat in the yogurt mixture. Check seasoning, and sprinkle with the chives. Serve piping hot.

SERVES: 4

TIME: Preparation takes 15 minutes, plus overnight soaking; cooking takes 1½ hours.

TAPENADE

INGREDIENTS
12 anchovy fillets in oil
115 g/4 oz pitted black olives
½ clove garlic
Pepper
4 tbsp capers
8 slices of toast

SERVES: 4

TIME: Preparation takes 15 minutes.

1 Remove the bones from the anchovy fillets and place the fillets in a mortar or heavy bowl.

2 Add the olives, garlic and pepper to taste and pound the mixture well until a smooth paste is obtained. It might be necessary to do this in 2 or 3 stages.

3 Mix the capers through the paste and spread on the slices of toast.

Cook's tip: 1 tbsp mayonnaise can be added to the paste to make it easier to spread.

Variation: Use green olives, or a mixture of green and black olives.

CHICKPEA BALLS

Cooked chickpeas, herbs and spice balls are deep-fried in oil and served with lemon in this tasty Israeli starter.

INGREDIENTS
460 g/1 lb cooked chickpeas
1 tbsp finely chopped onion
½ tsp finely chopped garlic
1 tbsp chopped parsley
Pinch ground cumin
Pinch chilli powder
Salt and pepper
1 egg, beaten
Oil for deep frying

1 Press the chickpeas through a metal sieve with a rigid spatula.

2 Add the onion, garlic, parsley, cumin, chilli powder, salt and pepper to the chickpea purée. Add the egg and beat the mixture well.

3 Form the mixture into even-sized small balls. Allow the balls to rest for 15 minutes.

4 Heat the oil to approximately 180°C/350°F. Plunge in the balls a few at a time. When crisp and golden brown, drain on kitchen paper and serve warm with lemon wedges.

Serving idea: The chickpea balls are delicious served with a lettuce salad tossed in olive oil vinaigrette.

Cook's tip: Flour your hands well to form the balls.

Checkpoint: The chickpeas must be well cooked and cold before being used in this recipe.

SERVES: 4

TIME: Preparation takes 45 minutes. Each batch takes about 4-5 minutes to cook.

Far left: **Chickpea Balls.**
Left: **The Garden of Gethsemane and the Church of All Nations in Jerusalem.**

CARPACCIO WITH CAPERS

Capers and fresh beef — an amazing Italian combination that provides a nourishing start to any meal.

INGREDIENTS

460 g/1 lb fillet steak

2 tbsp olive oil

1 squeeze lemon juice

2 tbsp capers

Salt and pepper

1 onion, chopped

SERVES: 6

TIME: Preparation takes about 30 minutes.

Variation: A little of the vinegar from the jar of capers may be used to replace the lemon juice in this recipe.

Watchpoint: It is very important to use finest quality, tender beef for this recipe. A cut from the centre of the fillet is best.

1 Cut the beef into very thin slices and spread them out on a serving plate.

2 Mix together the oil, lemon juice and the capers.

3 Season the beef with plenty of pepper and a little salt. Sprinkle over the onion, then pour the sauce over the beef.

4 Allow to marinate for at least 10 minutes before serving. Serve at room temperature.

Right: **Carpaccio with Capers, an unusual starter from Italy.**
Below: **The tiny fishing village of Riomaggiore near La Spezia, northwestern Italy, dates back to medieval times.**

Stuffed Eggs

Ingredients

6 eggs

200 g tin tuna in water, roughly chopped

15 leaves fresh basil, cut into very
thin strips

1 clove garlic, finely chopped

3 tbsp mayonnaise

1 tbsp finely chopped olives

Salt and pepper

Serves: 4

Time: Preparation takes 35 minutes and
cooking takes 10 minutes.

1 Cook the eggs in boiling water for
10 minutes. Drain off the water and
freshen the eggs in cold water.

2 Shell the eggs and cut them in half.
Remove the yolks and mix with the
tuna, basil and garlic. Gradually add the
mayonnaise, mixing well until a smooth
stuffing mixture is obtained.

3 Season the stuffing with salt and
pepper. Place in a piping bag with a
wide nozzle. Fill each egg half and
sprinkle over the chopped olives to
decorate. Serve slightly chilled.

MELON, FIGS AND PARMA HAM

INGREDIENTS
2 ripe melons

8 fresh figs

4 slices paper thin Parma
ham

Pepper

SERVES: 4

TIME: Preparation takes
about 20 minutes.

1 Peel the melons, cut them into quarters and remove the seeds.

2 Cut the figs in half lengthways with a sharp knife, then into quarters.

3 Spread the ingredients out attractively on a serving plate, sprinkling the melon pieces with a little pepper.

SPRATS IN MAYONNAISE

INGREDIENTS
550 g/1¼ lb sprats

1 carrot

1 sprig rosemary

Small bunch parsley

1 bay leaf

Salt and pepper

1 egg yolk

1 tsp mustard

1 clove garlic, chopped

100 ml/4 fl oz olive oil

1 Make a vegetable stock by boiling together in a large saucepan of water the carrot, rosemary, parsley and the bay leaf. Season well with salt and pepper, and simmer gently until the liquid is well flavoured.

2 Strain the stock through a fine sieve into a clean saucepan, then bring the stock to a gentle simmer and add the fish. Cook for about 2 minutes (longer if you prefer your fish very well cooked). Drain and set the fish aside to cool.

3 To make the mayonnaise, beat together the egg yolk, mustard, salt, pepper and garlic, then add the olive oil drop by drop, beating continuously.

4 Serve the fish hot or cold with the mayonnaise.

SERVES: 4

TIME: Preparation takes about 20 minutes and cooking takes about 5 minutes.

TOAST WITH AUBERGINE PURÉE

INGREDIENTS

2 aubergines, peeled and diced
2 tbsp olive oil
1 tbsp lemon juice
Pinch cardamom powder
Salt
2 cloves garlic, finely chopped
1 tbsp sesame seeds
8 slices toast, cut into small pieces

1 Heat the olive oil and gently fry the aubergine with the lemon juice. Cover and cook for 20 minutes, stirring frequently. When cooked, transfer the aubergine to a bowl to cool. Add the garlic.

2 Crush small amounts of the aubergine at a time, using a pestle or heavy spoon, until a smooth purée is obtained. Season with cardamom and salt.

3 Spread onto the small pieces of toast, sprinkle over the sesame seeds and serve.

SERVES: 4

TIME: Preparation takes about 25 minutes and cooking takes about 20 minutes.

HADDOCK MOUSSE

A delicious French mousse, delicately flavoured by the smoked haddock.

INGREDIENTS

3 sheets gelatine

3 smoked haddock fillets

220 ml/8 fl oz fish stock

180 ml/6 fl oz double cream

1 tbsp chopped chives

Salt and pepper

SERVES: 4

1 Soak the gelatine in a bowl of cold water. Set aside. Cut one of the fillets in half and chop it finely.

2 In a saucepan, gently heat the fish stock and chopped haddock fillet. Drain the gelatine sheets and stir into the stock until they have completely dissolved. Remove from the heat, transfer to a clean bowl and put in the refrigerator.

3 Meanwhile, whip the cream until it becomes light and fluffy. Keep cool.

4 Once the stock is completely cool, gently fold in the whipped cream, chives, salt and pepper. Return the mixture to the refrigerator for at least 2 hours.

5 Cut the remaining fillets into long slices and spread them out onto cling film. Place spoonfuls of mousse down the centre of each. There should be some mousse still left.

6 Gently roll up the slices of haddock to make neat rolls. Wrap the rolls in cling film and place in the refrigerator for a few hours to 'set'.

7 Using a teaspoon, form the remaining mousse into small oblong shapes and serve with the haddock roll.

TIME: Preparation takes about 1 hour, plus about 4 hours chilling.

*Left: **Many chateaux in France are also top-class hotels offering excellent cuisine.***

BEAN SOUP WITH SAFFRON

An easy and versatile North African soup that can be made using virtually any variety of dried beans.

INGREDIENTS

2 tbsp olive oil

1 onion, chopped

280 g/10 oz beans (soaked overnight)

1.8 litres/3 pints chicken stock

Salt and pepper

2 eggs

Pinch saffron

1 Heat the oil and gently fry the onion. Add the drained beans, fry for one minute then pour over the stock. Season with salt and pepper and cook for 1-1½ hours, until the beans are ready.

2 Beat the eggs with a fork. When the soup is cooked, remove from the heat, add the eggs and beat well.

3 Sprinkle the soup with saffron and serve immediately.

Variation: Try different beans, such as butter, black-eyed or haricot. Chickpeas are also good.

Cook's tip: The beaten egg mixture should be poured in one long stream over the boiling hot soup to create strings of coagulated egg.

Serving idea: Serve with croutons rubbed with a clove of garlic.

SERVES: 4

TIME: Preparation takes about 20 minutes, plus overnight soaking. Cooking takes about 1½ hours.

*Left: **A timeless scene on the Nile as vessels tack between sandy shores.***

TORTILLA

INGREDIENTS

120 ml/4 fl oz olive oil

225 g/½ lb potatoes, peeled and thinly sliced

Salt and pepper

1 large onion, thinly sliced

4 eggs

2 tomatoes, peeled, seeded and roughly chopped

2 spring onions, chopped

SERVES: 4-6

1 Heat the oil in a large frying pan and add the potatoes. Sprinkle lightly with salt and pepper, and cook over medium heat until slightly brown.

2 Add the onion and turn the potatoes and onions over occasionally to brown evenly – this takes about 20 minutes.

3 Beat the eggs with a pinch of salt and pepper, stir the potatoes and onions into the eggs and pour the mixture back into the pan. Cook over gentle heat until the bottom browns lightly.

4 Invert a large plate over the top of the pan and carefully turn the omelette out onto it. Slide the omelette back into the pan so the uncooked side has a chance to brown. Cook until the eggs are set.

5 Garnish with the tomatoes and spring onions, slice and serve warm.

TIME: Preparation takes 30 minutes and cooking takes 30-40 minutes.

ANCHOYADE

INGREDIENTS

15 salted anchovy fillets

2 cloves garlic

120 ml/4 fl oz olive oil

Few drops lemon juice

TO SERVE:

Mixed lettuce leaves

4 tbsp vinaigrette dressing

Slices French bread, toasted

1 Rinse the anchovy fillets under cold running water to remove the excess salt. Pat them dry on kitchen paper.

2 Pound the garlic with a pestle until smooth. Add the fillets and pound into the garlic until smooth.

3 Beat in the oil, a little at a time, until a smooth paste is formed. Spread the mixture onto the slices of toast.

4 Toss the lettuce in the vinaigrette dressing and place the toast slices on top.

SERVES: 6

TIME: Preparation takes 25 minutes.

Preparation: The anchoyade can be made in a blender – put all the ingredients in together and blend until smooth.

STUFFED PEPPERS

Peppers are stuffed with a minced lamb filling in this dish from Libya.

INGREDIENTS

12 small peppers

30 g/1 oz fresh breadcrumbs

A little milk

550 g/1¼ lb lamb (shoulder), cut into small cubes

1 tbsp chopped parsley

1 egg

1 tsp turmeric

Salt and pepper

115 g/4 oz cooked rice

2 tbsp olive oil

SERVES: 6

TIME: Preparation takes 30 minutes and cooking takes approximately 30 minutes.

1 Cut the tops off the peppers (retain them for later) and remove the pith and seeds. Try to keep the peppers whole.

2 Soak the breadcrumbs in the milk. Squeeze out the excess milk, then place the meat and soaked breadcrumbs in a food processor with the parsley, egg, turmeric, salt and pepper. Blend until smooth, then add the rice.

3 Precook the peppers in boiling, salted water for 4 minutes. Drain and dry with a tea towel. Stuff the peppers with the filling using a teaspoon.

4 Spread a little olive oil in the bottom of an ovenproof dish, add the stuffed peppers and sprinkle the remaining oil over the peppers.

5 Put the tops back on each pepper and cook them in a preheated 200°C/ 400°F/gas mark 6 oven for 25 minutes.

Above left: **Unlike the French omelette, the Spanish** tortilla **is not folded so it is easier to prepare.**
Left: **Stuffed Peppers.**

Cheese Bricks

Pasta dough is stuffed with a thick, cheese filling and deep-fried in this delicious Turkish recipe.

Ingredients

225 g/8 oz fresh lasagne sheets

175 g/6 oz cottage cheese or thick fromage frais

2 tbsp bechamel sauce

115 g/4 oz grated cheese

1 egg, beaten

2 tbsp finely chopped fresh herbs

Salt and pepper

Oil for deep frying

Serves: 4

Time: Preparation takes about 1 hour and cooking takes approximately 10-15 minutes, depending on how many batches are cooked.

Above right: **Tombs dating from the fourth century BC in the form of temple façades at Myra, Turkey.**

1 Prepare the stuffing by mixing together the cottage cheese, bechamel sauce, grated cheese, half of the egg and the fresh herbs. Season with salt and pepper.

2 Cut the pasta sheets into rectangles. Brush the remaining egg over each of the rectangles.

3 Place a little stuffing on one half of each rectangle, fold the other side of the rectangle over the stuffing and pinch all around the edges firmly with your fingers to seal the edges well.

4 Heat the oil to 175°C/340°F. Drop in a few bricks at a time, cooking them for approximately 2 minutes. Drain on kitchen paper.

5 Keep the first batches warm and serve the bricks hot.

Variation: Try chives, coriander, anise, etc., to flavour the filling.

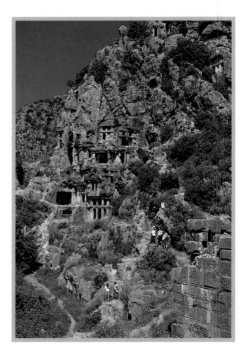

Cook's tip: Do not wait too long between the preparation of the bricks and cooking them, otherwise the stuffing will soak through the dough.

TRIPE SOUP

Tripe deserves a try if not already appreciated. This delicious, nutritious and low-calorie soup is from Tunisia.

INGREDIENTS

1.15 kg/2½ lb tripe, cleaned
4 tbsp olive oil
1 clove garlic, chopped
Peel of 1 orange
10 coriander seeds
1 bay leaf
1 tsp hot pepper paste (*harissa*)
1 bouquet garni
Cumin to taste
Salt and pepper
1 carrot
1 courgette

SERVES: 4

TIME: Preparation takes about 30 minutes and cooking takes at least 6 hours.

Above right: **Under the hot North African sun, life seems to move at a slower pace, allowing time to enjoy the company of friends and, of course, the delights of good food and drink.**

1 Place the cleaned tripe on the work surface and cut into slices with a sharp knife.

2 Heat the olive oil and fry the garlic, orange peel, coriander seeds and tripe for 2 minutes.

3 Cover completely with water and add the bay leaf, hot pepper paste, bouquet garni, cumin, salt and pepper. Cook on a very low heat for 6 hours.

4 Dice the carrot and courgette and add to the soup for the last 30 minutes of cooking.

SHORBA

A hearty and filling Algerian soup for cold winter evenings.

INGREDIENTS

460 g/1 lb lamb (shoulder or leg)

2 tbsp olive oil

1 onion, diced

175 g/6 oz broad beans, pre-soaked

175 g/6 oz chickpeas, pre-soaked

Salt and pepper

1 turnip, diced

1 carrot, diced

1 courgette, diced

10 coriander seeds

1 tomato, diced

55g/2 oz dried pasta shells

SERVES: 4

TIME: Preparation takes about 30 minutes, plus overnight soaking. Cooking takes about 1 hour and 30 minutes.

1 Cut the meat into small cubes. Heat the olive oil and gently fry the onion and meat together.

2 Add pre-soaked, rinsed and well-drained beans and chickpeas. Season with salt and pepper, then pour over sufficient water to just cover the ingredients. Cook for 45 minutes.

3 Add the diced vegetables (except the tomato) and coriander seeds. Cook for a further 10 minutes.

4 Add the tomato and pasta; check and adjust the seasoning. Cook for 10 minutes more and serve hot.

Variation: Shorba is a country dish that uses whatever vegetables are available, so vary the ingredients with the seasons.

Above left: **Tripe Soup.**
Left: **The ingredients for Shorba.**

Salads, Vegetables & Accompaniments

The baking sun and thin soils of many Mediterranean countries mean that there is only limited grazing land to support a fully-fledged meat industry. The alternative, however, is fortunately very healthy, with the peoples of the region enjoying a wide variety of vegetables. This bias shows itself in many delightful salads and side dishes, and when these are made with ingredients such as olive oil, garlic, beans and rice, it is recognised as helping to provide a beneficial diet.

Above: **Fresh fruit for the market.**
Left: **View at Ravello, Italy, from the 13th-century Villa Rufolo, once residence to several popes, Charles of Anjou and, in 1880, Wagner.**

CAULIFLOWER WITH ANCHOVIES

This Libyan dish is best served chilled, either as part of a buffet or as a starter to a summer meal.

INGREDIENTS

½ cauliflower

4 small potatoes

5 anchovy fillets

1 clove garlic

½ tsp hot pepper paste (*harissa*), diluted with 1 tbsp water

1 tbsp olive oil

10 coriander seeds

1 tbsp finely chopped fresh coriander

2 tbsp water

Salt and pepper

SERVES: 4

TIME: Preparation takes about 30 minutes and cooking takes about 30 minutes in total.

Right: Fruit and vegetables are still sold at the wayside in North Africa as they have been for millennia.

1 Cut the cauliflower into small pieces, discarding any hard stalks.

2 Steam or gently simmer the unpeeled potatoes until just tender. Drain.

3 Cook the cauliflower in salted, boiling water until crisp-tender. Drain.

4 Remove and discard any bones from the anchovy fillets, and crush the fillets with the garlic and hot pepper paste. Continue until the ingredients are smoothly blended and well combined.

5 Peel the potatoes and cut into small cubes. Heat the oil and sauté the cauliflower and potato over a moderately high heat.

6 Add the anchovy paste mixture to the pan. Sprinkle over the coriander seeds and fresh coriander. Stir in the 2 tbsp water, season with salt and pepper, and cook for 1 minute.

7 Serve either hot or cold.

Variation: This dish is traditionally quite spicy. Augment or diminish the amount of hot pepper paste according to personal taste.

Watchpoint: At step 6, the oil should be hot and the vegetables dry, or at least well drained.

SALAD NIÇOISE

This French salad is a marvellous mixture of fresh vegetables, lettuce and eggs in a vinaigrette dressing.

INGREDIENTS

2 eggs

2 potatoes

115 g/4 oz green beans

2 tomatoes

1 large onion

½ red pepper

½ green pepper

2 tbsp lemon juice

Salt and pepper

2 tbsp olive oil

4 small servings of mixed
   lettuce leaves

10 anchovy fillets

1 tbsp chopped olives

SERVES: 4

TIME: **Preparation takes 40 minutes and cooking about 20 minutes.**

1 Cook the eggs in boiling water for 10 minutes. Freshen under cold water and shell them.

2 Cook the potatoes in slightly salted boiling water until cooked through. Freshen in cold water and then peel. Cut the potatoes into thick slices.

3 Cook the beans in salted, boiling water for 7-10 minutes. Check by tasting after 7 minutes; they should be crisp-tender. Set aside to drain.

4 Cut the tomatoes and onion into round slices (quite thin for the onion). Cut the peppers into thin matchsticks.

5 Make the sauce by mixing together the lemon juice, salt, pepper and olive oil. Set the sauce aside.

6 Cut the egg into round slices and then into small cubes.

7 Mix together the cooled ingredients and vegetables and add the lettuce, anchovies, olives, salt and pepper. Serve with the sauce.

Avocado Salad

Ingredients

2 ripe avocados
4 tbsp lemon juice
1 tbsp chopped olives
1 tbsp crushed walnuts
5 coriander seeds, crushed
1 tsp mustard
Salt and pepper
3 tbsp olive oil

Serves: 4
Time: Preparation takes 30 minutes.

1 Cut the avocados in half lengthways, remove the stones and peel off the skin. Sprinkle over a little of the lemon juice. Cut the avocados into thin slices, sprinkling over a little more lemon juice to avoid discolouring.

2 To make the sauce, mix together 2 tbsp lemon juice, the chopped olives, walnuts, coriander seeds and mustard. Season, then beat in the olive oil.

3 Serve the sauce spooned over the avocados, or in a small bowl for guests to help themselves.

ARTICHOKE HEART SALAD

INGREDIENTS

4 artichokes

1 lemon

Juice of 1 lemon

Salt and pepper

Paprika

2 tbsp olive oil

2 tbsp chopped black olives

SERVES: 4

1 Trim off all the leaves from the artichokes to obtain 4 artichoke hearts. Cook the hearts in salted, boiling water (to which you have added a little lemon juice) for about 30 minutes or until tender.

2 Drain the hearts and cut out the 'bearded' centre part. Cut into thin slices.

3 Prepare a vinaigrette by mixing together the lemon juice, salt, pepper and a little paprika. Beat in the olive oil, then add the olives.

4 Serve the sliced artichoke hearts with the vinaigrette poured over.

TIME: Preparation takes 70 minutes and cooking takes about 35 minutes.

AVOCADO, ORANGE AND BLACK OLIVE SALAD

INGREDIENTS

2 oranges, peeled and segmented

2 avocados

20 black olives, pitted

Basil leaves

½ small red onion, thinly sliced

DRESSING:

1 tbsp white wine or sherry vinegar

4 tbsp olive oil

½ tsp mustard

Pinch salt and pepper

1 Make sure all the white pith is removed from each segment of orange. Cut the avocados in half and remove the stones. Peel them and cut the flesh into slices.

2 Cut the olives in half. Use kitchen scissors to shred the basil leaves finely.

3 Arrange the orange segments, avocado slices, sliced onion and olives on serving plates and sprinkle over the shredded basil leaves. Mix the dressing ingredients together well and pour over the salad to serve.

Cook's tip: Do not peel the avocados more than 30 minutes before serving unless you prepare the dressing beforehand and coat the avocados with it to prevent discoloration.

Variation: Spring onions may be used instead of the red onions. Use different varieties of herbs. Substitute grapefruit for the orange.

SERVES: 4

TIME: Preparation takes about 30 minutes.

VEGETABLE AND EGG ASPICS

In this Balkan dish decorative aspics are made with vegetables, quail eggs and pretty courgette flowers.

INGREDIENTS

½ courgette

1 large carrot

115 g/4 oz green beans

½ stick celery

115 g/4 oz peas

8 quail eggs

1½ packets powdered gelatine, softened in a little cold water

55 ml/2 fl oz chicken stock

Salt and pepper

8 courgette flowers

SERVES: 4

TIME: **Preparation takes about 45 minutes and chilling time is at least 2 hours.**

1 Cut the courgette, carrot, green beans and celery into small cubes.

2 Cook all the vegetables in salted, boiling water, separately, not forgetting the courgette flowers (if available). Freshen under cold water and set aside to drain.

3 Cook the eggs in boiling water for 1 minute, freshen in cold water and shell them carefully.

4 Drain the gelatine. Heat the stock and stir in the softened gelatine. Remove from the heat as soon as the gelatine dissolves. Season with salt and pepper.

5 Place a little of the stock in the bottom of 8 ramekin or aspic moulds. Place the molds in the refrigerator for 10 minutes. Place a courgette flower in the mould over the stock base.

6 Mix together all the cooked vegetables and fill each mould halfway with this mixture.

7 Place an egg in the centre of the vegetable mixture, pushing it down slightly. Spoon over a little more vegetable mixture and then cover with the remaining stock.

8 Place in the refrigerator for 2 hours before serving. Serve turned out on a serving plate.

Truffle Risotto

Ingredients
2 medium truffles
30 g/1 oz butter
1 small onion, finely chopped
1 thick-cut bacon rasher
460 g/1 lb rice
750 ml/26 fl oz chicken stock
Salt and pepper

Serves: 4

Time: Preparation takes about 8 minutes and total cooking time is approximately 25 minutes.

1 Using a small very sharp knife, cut the truffles into thin slices.

2 Melt the butter in a large saucepan, add the onion and, when it just begins to soften, stir in the bacon and rice. Stir well and cook for 1 minute.

3 Add the truffles and pour over the stock. Season with salt and pepper.

4 Transfer to an ovenproof dish and cook, covered, in a preheated 200°C/400°F/gas mark 6 oven for about 20 minutes. Serve immediately.

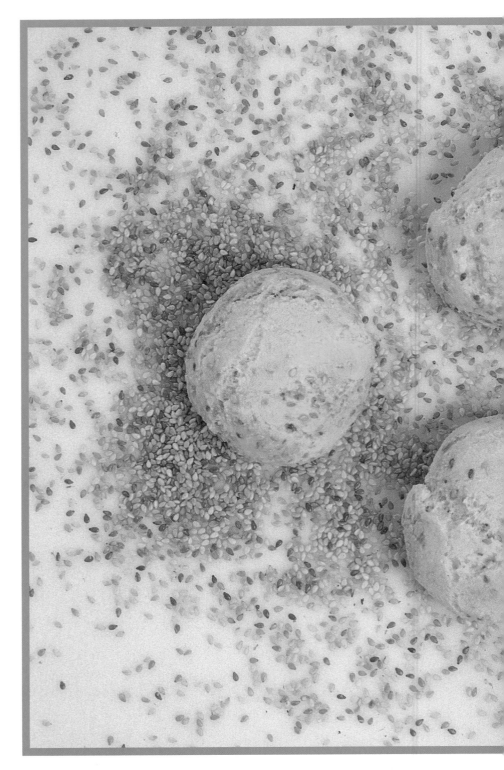

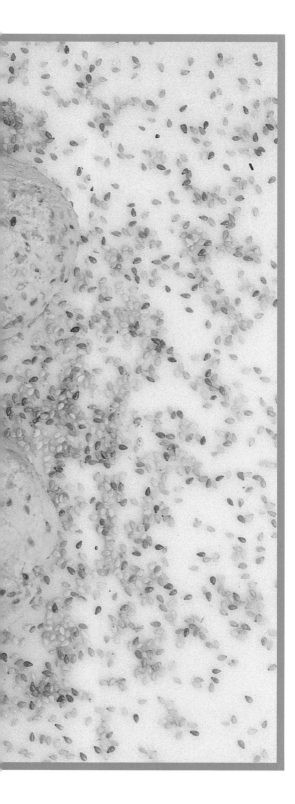

*Left: **Semolina Rolls, a favourite from the shores of North Africa.***

SEMOLINA ROLLS

These small Algerian rolls give an extra touch to a special meal.

INGREDIENTS

1 tsp yeast
2 tsp olive oil
140 g/5 oz medium semolina
115 ml/4 fl oz water
2 tbsp sesame seeds (optional)
1 egg, beaten

SERVES: 4

TIME: Preparation takes
15 minutes, resting time is
1 hour and 30 minutes, and
cooking takes 20 minutes.

Cook's tip: The sesame
seeds are optional. Brown
lightly in a hot oven for
2 minutes before use to
enhance their flavour.

1 Stir the yeast into 4 tsp warm, lightly salted water.

2 Stir the olive oil into the semolina, add the yeast and water mixture, and stir well. Add the remaining water to the mixture, little by little, stirring well to combine the ingredients.

3 Place the dough in a clean bowl and cover with a tea towel. Keep in a warm place for 1 hour.

4 After 1 hour, mix the sesame seeds into the dough, mixing well. Roll small pieces of dough into the desired shape and brush a little of the egg over each roll using a pastry brush. Leave to rest for 30 minutes more in a warm place.

5 Place the rolls on an ungreased baking sheet and bake in a preheated 200°C/400°F/gas mark 6 oven for approximately 20 minutes.

Watchpoint: Resting time between steps is important for the yeast to react.

FRESH PASTA WITH CEPS

INGREDIENTS

460 g/1 lb fresh pasta

225 g/8 oz ceps

55 g/2 oz butter

½ tsp chopped garlic

Salt and pepper

1 tbsp chopped chives

SERVES: 4

TIME: Preparation takes about 20 minutes and cooking takes approximately 15 minutes.

1 Cook the pasta until tender in salted, boiling water. Drain, rinse in fresh water and set aside to drain.

2 Cut the stems off the ceps. Wash the mushrooms carefully and dry them well. Cut into very thin slices.

3 Heat half the butter and sauté the ceps with the garlic for 2 minutes. Season with plenty of salt and pepper.

4 Add the remaining butter to the pan. When it has melted, add the pasta, stir briskly and add the chives. Keep on the heat until the pasta is heated through completely and serve on preheated plates.

Cook's tip: Ceps can be found in good supermarkets, or can be replaced using chanterelle mushrooms.

*Right: **Fresh Pasta with Ceps** uses fungi that grow wild in the Mediterranean countryside.*

PAIN PERDU/FRENCH TOAST

INGREDIENTS

2 eggs

5 tbsp milk

1 tsp orange-flower water

8 slices white bread, crusts removed

55 g/2 oz butter

30-55 g/1-2 oz sugar

SERVES: 4

1 Beat the eggs with the milk and add the orange-flower water. Soak the slices of bread in the mixture.

2 Melt half the butter in a large frying pan and add 4 slices of bread to the pan.

3 Cook until browned lightly, turn the slices over and sprinkle over the sugar.

4 When the second side is slightly browned and crisp turn them over again to caramelise the sugared side lightly. Repeat with the remaining slices.

5 Serve hot or cold.

Cook's tip: Soak the slices in the egg mixture well, but not for too long, otherwise they become very soggy and impossible to handle.

Variation: If available, French brioche – a slightly sweet, yeast loaf – can be used.

TIME: Preparation takes 10 minutes and cooking takes about 10 minutes.

PEPPER SALAD

In this North African recipe, sweet red peppers are peeled
after baking and then sautéed with garlic in olive oil.

INGREDIENTS

3 red peppers
3 tbsp olive oil
1 tsp chopped garlic
2 tbsp wine vinegar
Salt and pepper
Few coriander seeds
SERVES: 4

1 Place the peppers in a greased
ovenproof dish and cook in a preheated
200°C/400°F/gas mark 6 oven for
15 minutes.

2 Remove the peppers from the oven,
wrap them in a tea towel and set aside
for 10 minutes. Using a small sharp
knife, peel off the skins, taking care not
to tear the peppers. Cut the peppers
into even strips.

3 Heat the olive oil and sauté the
pepper strips with the garlic. Deglaze
the pan rapidly with the vinegar.
Season with salt, pepper and coriander
seeds, and set aside to cool.

4 Serve either warm, at room
temperature or chilled from the
refrigerator.

Serving idea: Sprinkle with a little
finely chopped, fresh chives and serve
with a tossed green salad.

TIME: Preparation takes about
25 minutes and cooking takes
approximately 15 minutes. If serving
chilled, allow an extra 30 minutes.

Left: **An Arab woman carefully examines
produce before deciding to buy.**
Opposite page, top: **Pepper Salad.**

TCHAKCHOUKA

This spicy Algerian ratatouille is flavoured with garlic and chilli powder.

INGREDIENTS

4 tomatoes

2 green peppers, seeded

3 tbsp olive oil

1 onion, chopped

1 clove garlic, chopped

1 bouquet garni (parsley, bay leaf, thyme)

Pinch chilli powder

Salt and pepper

SERVES: 4

TIME: Preparation takes about 20 minutes and cooking takes approximately 35 minutes.

Left: Fried in olive oil then stewed slowly with an aromatic mixture of spices, Tchakchouka makes a delightful vegetable casserole. For an unusual presentation, mould into oblong shapes.

1 Cut out the stalks from the tomatoes, plunge into boiling water for 10 seconds, then immediately into cold water. Peel with the tip of a sharp knife. Cut in half and remove the juice and the pips. Chop the tomato flesh and set aside.

2 Cut the peppers into even-sized small cubes.

3 Heat the oil and fry the peppers, onion and garlic together for 3 minutes. Add the tomato flesh and the bouquet garni, chilli powder, salt and pepper to taste.

4 Cook on a gentle heat, stirring from time to time, for approximately 20-30 minutes. Remove the bouquet garni and serve hot or cold.

Cook's tip: This ratatouille should be thick, with very little liquid left in the pan. If not reduced after 30 minutes, continue cooking over a higher heat until the liquid evaporates.

FISHERMAN'S SALAD

A new dish from France that makes a perfect light lunch or an elegant starter.

INGREDIENTS

1 carrot, scraped

½ cucumber, peeled and seeded

1 red pepper, seeded

1 courgette

About 40 small cooked shrimp, peeled (retain peelings)

1 tbsp olive oil

1 tbsp brandy or cognac

150 ml/5 fl oz single cream

Juice of ½ lemon

2 tbsp chopped chervil

SERVES: 4

TIME: Preparation takes about 35 minutes.

1 Cut each of the vegetables carefully into thin strips. As you finish each vegetable, put the strips in the refrigerator to keep them crisp and fresh.

2 Fry the shrimp peelings briskly over a high heat for 5 minutes in the olive oil. Add the brandy or cognac and flambé the mixture. Allow the alcohol to burn out, then stir in the cream and continue cooking over a low heat for about 10 minutes.

3 Strain the sauce through a fine sieve, discarding all but the smooth sauce. Blend the sauce with a hand mixer and then put the sauce in the refrigerator to cool.

4 Spread a single bed of the vegetable strips on a serving dish and sprinkle over the peeled shrimp.

5 Add the lemon juice to the cooled sauce, stir well and pour it over the salad. Sprinkle with chervil and serve.

Above: **The scenic harbour at Cassis, which lies to the southeast of Marseille, France.**

Cook's tip: The sauce can be made in advance and kept in the refrigerator.

Preparation: Vegetables can be prepared on the morning of serving and kept covered in the refrigerator.

TOMATO AND MOZZARELLA SALAD

INGREDIENTS.
1 ball fresh mozzarella
1 tbsp mature wine vinegar
2½ tbsp olive oil
Salt and pepper
Handful fresh basil leaves
4 tomatoes, sliced

1 Drain the mozzarella and cut into even slices.

2 Mix together the vinegar and olive oil. Season with salt and pepper.

3 Cut the basil leaves into thin strips and add to the dressing (save a little to sprinkle over for decoration).

4 Interlace the tomato and mozzarella slices attractively on a serving plate, pour over the dressing and scatter the reserved basil over the top.

SERVES: 4

TIME: Preparation takes about 15 minutes.

Cook's tip: Do not use very fresh mozzarella as it has a tendency to crumble when you try to slice it.

RICE WITH HERBS

INGREDIENTS
10 mint leaves
10 sprigs chive
Small bunch dill
Small bunch chervil
2 tbsp olive oil
1 onion, chopped
225 g/8 oz rice
340 ml/12 fl oz water or stock
Salt and pepper

SERVES: 4

1 Chop all the herbs very finely and set them aside.

2 In an ovenproof pan, gently fry the onion in the oil. Add the rice, frying until the rice becomes transparent.

3 Sprinkle the herbs over the rice. Pour over the water, season with salt and pepper. Cover and cook in a preheated 200°C/400°F/gas mark 6 oven for 20 minutes. Serve hot.

Checkpoint: When frying the rice, stir continuously for 1 minute until transparent, then pour over the liquid. Do not stir after this stage until cooked.

Variation: Dried herbs can be used, but reduce the quantities as they tend to have stronger flavours.

TIME: Preparation takes 10 minutes and cooking takes about 20 minutes.

Buckwheat Polenta

Ingredients

600 ml/1 pint milk

140 g/5 oz buckwheat flour

30 g/1 oz butter, cubed

2 tbsp grated cheese (Cheddar or similar)

Salt and pepper

Serves: 4

Time: Preparation takes 5 minutes and cooking takes about 35 minutes.

1 Bring the milk to the boil in a large saucepan. Add the buckwheat flour gradually, stirring with a wooden spoon to obtain a thick mixture. Reduce the heat to low and continue stirring for 30 minutes.

2 At the end of 30 minutes, stir in the butter, grated cheese, salt and pepper. Cook for 5 minutes, stirring well, and serve hot.

Left: Buckwheat Polenta, a savoury Balkan dish to accompany a rich meal.

SAVOURY FRESH FRUIT SALAD

INGREDIENTS

½ cucumber

2 tbsp lemon juice

Pinch salt, pepper and cumin

½ tsp orange-flower water

4 tbsp olive oil

4 oranges, peeled and
    segmented

10 dates, chopped

4 small servings of mixed
    lettuce

1 tbsp chopped black olives

SERVES: 4

TIME: Preparation takes 35 minutes.

1 Slice the cucumber lengthways in two and scoop out the seeds. Cut the cucumber into half-moon shaped slices.

2 Make the sauce by mixing together the lemon juice, salt, pepper, cumin, orange-flower water and olive oil.

3 Place the lettuce on a serving dish and lay the cucumber on top with the orange segments. Sprinkle over the dates and olives, season with salt and pepper and serve with the sauce.

Right: **Savoury Fresh Fruit Salad.**

RICE WITH DATES

INGREDIENTS

20 dates

2 tbsp olive oil

1 onion, chopped

225 g/8 oz rice

Salt and pepper

½ tsp cumin

SERVES: 4

1 Cut the dates into thin crossways slices.

2 Heat the olive oil and fry the onion and the dates.

3 Add the rice and cook for a few moments until transparent. Pour over 570 ml/20 fl oz water. Season with salt, pepper and cumin.

4 Place the mixture in an ovenproof dish, cover and cook in a 180°C/350°F/gas mark 4 oven for 20 minutes. Serve hot.

Serving idea: This rice goes well with a spicy meat dish.

Time: Preparation takes about 20 minutes and cooking takes 20 minutes.

TABBOULEH

A Lebanese salad of semolina with tomatoes, peppers, cucumber, olives, parsley, mint, lemon juice and olive oil.

INGREDIENTS

225 g/8 oz semolina

Salt and pepper

2 tomatoes, cubed

½ green pepper, cubed

½ red pepper, cubed

¼ cucumber, peeled and cubed

1 onion, finely chopped

Small bunch parsley, very finely chopped

10 leaves fresh mint, very finely chopped

2 tbsp chopped black olives

Juice of 1 lemon

2 tbsp olive oil

SERVES: 4

TIME: Preparation takes about 40 minutes in total and chilling takes at least 2 hours.

1 Place the semolina in a bowl and add just enough water to cover. Season with salt and pepper. Set aside until the semolina has completely absorbed all the water (approximately 20 minutes).

2 When the water has been absorbed, add the cubed vegetables, herbs, olives, lemon juice and olive oil. Stir well and add salt and pepper to taste.

3 Chill in the refrigerator for at least 2 hours before serving, stirring occasionally.

Serving idea: Reserve a spoonful of each of the cubed vegetables to garnish the finished dish.

Variation: Try using lime juice instead of lemon.

Cook's tip: Leave the tabbouleh for 24 hours in the refrigerator for the flavour to develop fully. Tabbouleh should be eaten within 2 days of preparation.

MARINATED BEETROOTS

INGREDIENTS

4 beetroots, cooked

3 tbsp olive oil

1 tsp chopped garlic

1 shallot, chopped

2 pinches paprika

2 tbsp vinegar

Salt and pepper

SERVES: 4

TIME: **Preparation takes about 30 minutes, cooking takes 5 minutes and marinating at least 6 hours.**

1 Peel the beetroots and cut them into slices. Heat the olive oil, add the garlic and shallot and gently fry for 2 minutes. Place the beetroot slices on top and continue cooking for 1 minute. Turn the slices over and cook for 1 minute more. Sprinkle with paprika.

2 Deglaze with the vinegar and season with salt and pepper. Turn the contents of the pan into a shallow bowl and marinate in the refrigerator for at least 6 hours.

MARINATED TURNIPS

INGREDIENTS

3 long turnips

Juice of 2 lemons

½ tsp hot pepper paste
(*harissa*)

1 tbsp finely chopped parsley

1 tbsp chopped chives

½ tsp finely chopped garlic

1 tbsp wine vinegar

Salt

SERVES: 4

1 Peel and cut the turnips into thin, even-sized slices.

2 Mix together the lemon juice, hot pepper paste, parsley, chives, garlic and vinegar to make a marinade.

3 Place the slices of turnip on a plate and sprinkle over a little salt. Pour the marinade over the turnips and place in the refrigerator for 1 day, turning over from time to time.

Buying guide: Various types of turnips are available: round, white, purple and long. Long turnips, used in this recipe, are slightly sweeter than the others.

TIME: Preparation takes about 25 minutes. Allow 1 day for marinating.

Right: **Marinated Turnips – a Tunisian recipe.** *These thin slices are delicious served with crusty bread at apéritif time.*

ROAST PEPPER SALAD

INGREDIENTS

6 red peppers

6 tbsp olive oil

2 tbsp red or white wine vinegar

Salt and pepper

1 clove garlic, roughly chopped

1 spring onion, diagonally sliced

SERVES: 6

1 Preheat a grill and cut the peppers in half, removing the seeds, stems and cores. Flatten the peppers with the palm of your hand and brush the skin side of each pepper lightly with oil. Place the peppers under the grill.

2 Grill the peppers until the skins are well charred on top. Do not turn them.

3 Wrap the peppers in a clean tea towel and leave to stand for about 15-20 minutes.

4 Unwrap the peppers and peel off the skin using a small, sharp knife. Cut them into strips. Mix the remaining oil with the vinegar, salt and pepper. Place the peppers in a serving dish and pour over the dressing. Sprinkle over the garlic and spring onion and leave the peppers to stand for about 30 minutes before serving.

TIME: Preparation takes about 20 minutes. Grilling the peppers takes approximately 10-12 minutes.

RICE WITH TOMATO

This Egyptian recipe combines cooked rice with a spicy, slightly hot tomato sauce.

INGREDIENTS

2 tbsp olive oil

1 onion, chopped

225 g/8 oz long-grain rice

Turmeric

Salt and pepper

Chicken stock

600 ml/1 pint tomato sauce

1 tsp hot pepper paste (*harissa*)

1 Heat the oil and sauté the onion; do not allow it to brown. Add the rice and cook for 2 minutes, or until the rice becomes transparent.

2 Pour over sufficient stock or water – the equivalent of one and a half times the volume of rice – and season with the turmeric, salt and pepper to taste.

3 Place in an ovenproof casserole and cook, covered, in a preheated 200°C/400°F/gas mark 6 oven for 20 minutes, or until all the liquid is absorbed.

4 Heat the tomato sauce and add the hot pepper paste. Season with salt and pepper, if necessary.

5 Serve the rice with the tomato sauce in a sauce boat.

Variation: Try different kinds of rice for this dish, such as brown, wild, basmati, etc.

SERVES: 4

TIME: Preparation takes 5 minutes and cooking takes about 35 minutes.

Left: **The River Nile cuts a passage through the Egyptian desert, providing life-giving water to the vegetation that clings to its banks.**
Opposite page, top: **Rice with Tomato.**

CHICKPEA SALAD

This delicious marinated chickpea salad has its origins in Algeria.

INGREDIENTS

225 g/8 oz chickpeas, soaked
  for 2 hours in cold water
1 carrot, finely sliced
1 bouquet garni
1 onion, chopped
Salt and pepper
Pinch cumin powder
Pinch chilli powder
10 coriander seeds
2 tbsp olive oil
2 tbsp lemon juice

SERVES: 4

TIME: Preparation takes 15
minutes, plus 2 hours
soaking. Cooking takes
1 hour and 30 minutes and
marinating half a day.

Left: Chickpea Salad. Chickpeas have a nutty flavour and are widely used in stews across North Africa and into Spain.

1 Cook the chickpeas in salted, boiling water with the carrot and bouquet garni for approximately 1 hour and 30 minutes, testing from time to time for tenderness.

2 When the peas are cooked, drain, discarding the liquid, carrot and bouquet garni. Set the peas aside to cool.

3 Add the onion to the peas. Season with salt, pepper, cumin, chilli powder and the coriander seeds.

4 Pour over the lemon juice and the olive oil. Stir well to mix all the ingredients.

5 Leave to marinate for half a day and serve at room temperature.

Cook's tip: Tinned chickpeas can be used for this recipe. Rinse them well in cold water and drain, then continue from step 3.

Variation: Try different varieties of dried peas or beans in this dish, such as lentils or cannellini beans, etc.

EGYPTIAN SALAD

To enjoy it at its best, serve this delicious rice and chicken liver salad warm.

INGREDIENTS

4 chicken livers

Salt and pepper

Paprika

5 tbsp olive oil

2 tbsp lemon juice

225 g/8 oz cooked rice

55 g/2 oz cooked peas

1 red pepper, chopped

Saffron to taste

1 cooked artichoke heart

2 tomatoes

SERVES: 4

TIME: Preparation takes about 35 minutes and cooking takes approximately 5 minutes.

1 Sprinkle the chicken livers liberally with salt, pepper and paprika. Sauté the livers in 2 tbsp olive oil until well browned.

2 Mix together the lemon juice and a little paprika. Beat in the remaining olive oil to make a sauce.

3 Mix together the rice, peas and red pepper. Add 2 tbsp of the sauce, the saffron, salt and pepper. Mix well.

4 Cut the livers into thin, even-sized slices. Dice the artichoke hearts and tomatoes.

5 Spread the rice on a serving plate. Lay the livers over the rice, then the diced artichoke and tomatoes. Pour over the remaining sauce and serve.

Cook's tip: If the chicken livers are very thick, finish cooking in a hot oven for a few minutes.

Above: **Egypt's Sphinx: a mythological creature with a lion's body and a human head.**

Variation: Chicken livers can be replaced by veal's liver, but cooking time will be a little longer. Allow the livers to cool down to warm before serving them on the rice with the other ingredients.

Cook's tip: The saffron can be replaced by artificial food colouring.

Fish and Seafood

There is a wide variety of Mediterranean fish and shellfish suitable for eating, including red mullet, sea bass, squid, tuna, crab, mussels and prawns. Small oily fish thrive in the warm waters, and there is little more delightful than sitting down to enjoy a plate of freshly grilled, barbecued or stuffed sardines. A small-scale fishing industry flourishes along the Mediterranean littoral and tiny vessels, with their brightly coloured sides and sails, add a dashing gaiety to the cosy harbours. There is safe haven there at the end of the day not only for the boats, but also for the hungry in the friendly cafés, tavernas and restaurants that cluster round.

Above: **Fresh fish for sale in Turkey, straight from the sea.**
Left: **The picturesque fishing harbour at Agde, which lies to the southwest of Montpellier, France.**

ISRAELI-STYLE CARP

In this recipe slices of fresh carp are placed on a bed of garlic and onion, covered with fish stock and gently cooked.

INGREDIENTS

1 carp (weighing 1 kg/2¼ lb approximately)

3 tbsp olive oil

2 onions, finely sliced

1 tsp finely chopped garlic

115 ml/4 fl oz white wine

600 ml/1 pint fish stock

Salt and pepper

Chilli powder

1 bouquet garni

1 tsp plain flour

1 tbsp chopped fresh herbs (parsley, coriander, etc.)

SERVES: 4

TIME: Preparation takes about 30 minutes and cooking takes approximately 30 minutes.

1 Prepare the carp. Scrape off the scales and cut off the fins with scissors. Slice the carp open with a sharp knife and gut. Cut the carp into thick slices, using a serrated knife.

2 Heat the olive oil in a large frying pan and gently sauté the onions and garlic together.

3 Place the fish on the bed of onions and garlic in the pan. Add the wine and stock. Season with salt, pepper and chilli powder. Add the bouquet garni and the flour. Stir well, cover and cook for 20-30 minutes.

4 Remove the bouquet garni and the slices of fish. Keep the fish warm, discard the bouquet garni and allow the sauce in the pan to reduce. Serve the sauce spooned over the fish and decorate with the fresh herbs.

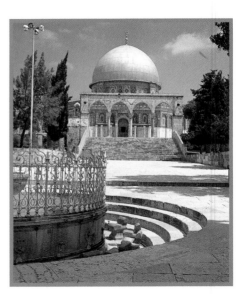

Above: **The Dome of the Rock, sacred to both Jews and Muslims, in Jerusalem.**

Serving idea: The fish can be served hot or cold. If cold, serve with a tossed mixed green salad.

AVGOLEMONO WITH FISH

This marvellous fish stock, enriched and thickened with eggs,
is perfect served as a winter warmer.

INGREDIENTS

1.6 kg/3½ lb various fish
  (with heads and bones, but
  gutted and rinsed)

2 tbsp olive oil

1 onion, sliced

1 carrot, sliced

½ leek, chopped

1 bouquet garni

115 ml/4 fl oz white wine

2 eggs

Juice of 1 lemon

Salt and pepper

2 tbsp finely chopped parsley

SERVES: 4

TIME: Preparation takes about
30 minutes and cooking takes
approximately 50 minutes.

1 Fry the whole fish in the olive oil for a few minutes each side. Add the onion, carrot, leek and bouquet garni. Deglaze with the white wine and heat until the wine has completely evaporated.

2 Pour over enough water to cover all the ingredients and cook for 45 minutes. Strain through a fine sieve and reserve 1.2 litres/32 fl oz of stock.

3 Whip the eggs and lemon juice together.

4 Bring the strained stock to the boil once again, then remove from the heat.

5 Place the egg and lemon mixture in a large bowl and gradually, whisking continuously, add the stock. The soup will become thick. Season with salt and pepper.

6 Dip the edges of 4 heat-resistant bowls in water and then in the chopped parsley. Pour the soup hot or cold into the decorated bowls and serve.

Checkpoint: The stock should be boiling hot when poured into the egg and lemon juice mixture. Whisk until thick.

Variation: In Greece during the hot months this soup is traditionally served iced, with a little more lemon juice added.

FRIED FISH IN A LIGHT BATTER

A light home-made batter makes an interesting and tasty Tunisian fish entrée that even children enjoy.

INGREDIENTS

4 whiting
175 g/6 oz plain flour
1 tsp yeast
115 ml/4 fl oz warm water
1 egg
55 g/2 fl oz oil
Pinch chilli powder
Salt and pepper
Oil for deep frying
2 lemons, cut into wedges

SERVES: 4

TIME: Preparation takes about 40 minutes, resting time for the batter is 1 hour and cooking takes 5 minutes.

1 Cut off the fillets from the whiting, making them into the shape desired.

2 Place the flour in a bowl and form a well in the centre. Dissolve the yeast in the warm water and add this to the flour with a good pinch of salt.

3 Add the egg and the oil, and mix well with your hands to blend all the flour and liquid. Leave the batter to rest for 1 hour.

4 Season the pieces of fish with chilli powder, salt and pepper.

5 Heat the oil to 180°C/350°F. Dip the fish in the batter and then drop the fish into the hot oil.

6 When crisp and golden, drain on kitchen paper. Serve with lemon wedges.

Cook's tip: The fish should not be too thick, so that it cooks through to the middle.

Serving idea: Serve the fish with a vinaigrette sauce, spiced with half a chilli pepper. Dip the fish into the sauce just before eating.

SQUID WITH TURNIPS

This Tunisian dish is an unusual combination of squid in a tomato sauce with turnips.

INGREDIENTS

8 medium squid

2 tbsp olive oil

2 shallots, finely chopped

4 tomatoes, peeled, seeded and blended smooth with a hand mixer

2 turnips, peeled and cut into small stick shapes

1 tsp hot pepper paste (*harissa*)

Salt and pepper

115 ml/4 fl oz rich fish stock (reduce 225 ml/8 fl oz to make rich fish stock)

3 sprigs chive

SERVES: 4

TIME: Preparation takes about 1 hour and cooking takes approximately 35 minutes.

Right: **The rocky island of Mykonos in the Cyclades, Greece.** *Opposite page:* **Squid with Turnips.**

1 Prepare the squid by first pulling off the skin covering the body. Cut off the head and the tentacles, pulling out the body sac. Wash the squid well in plenty of clean water (making sure the inside is well cleaned). Cut the body into thin slices.

2 Heat the olive oil and fry the sliced squid and the shallot for 1 minute.

3 Add the tomato purée and the turnips. Stir well and add the hot pepper paste, salt, pepper and fish stock.

4 Cover and cook for approximately 30 minutes on a gentle heat.

5 Serve hot, decorated with the sprigs of whole or chopped chives.

CRISPY GRILLED MACKEREL

INGREDIENTS

8 medium-sized fresh mackerel, gutted,
  washed and wiped dry
225 g/8 oz plain flour
120 ml/4 fl oz oil
Salt

TO SERVE:

2 lemons, washed, wiped and quartered
2 tbsp chopped parsley

SERVES: 4

TIME: Preparation takes 20 minutes and
cooking takes about 20 minutes.

1 Preheat the griddle or a frying pan until
very hot.

2 Ensure the mackerel are dried thoroughly
then roll each of the fish in the flour,
shaking off the excess.

3 Dip the floured fish quickly into the oil,
sprinkle over the salt, then place them on
the griddle or frying pan and cook until
crisp, about 15-20 minutes. Salt lightly
before serving.

RED MULLET WITH MAYONNAISE

This recipe can be served warm or cold for an authentic Syrian dish.

INGREDIENTS

8 red mullet

1 large slice bread, crusts removed

1 tsp pine nuts

1 egg yolk

1 tsp garlic, chopped

Pinch chilli powder

Salt and pepper

225 ml/8 fl oz olive oil

2 tbsp olive oil for frying

1 tbsp chopped chives

SERVES: 4

TIME: Preparation takes about 30 minutes and cooking takes approximately 5 minutes.

Variation: Any variety of whitefish can be used to replace the red mullet.

1 Cut the fillets off the fish. Rinse in cold water and dry with kitchen paper.

2 Soak the bread in a little water. Squeeze out the excess water and place the bread in a mortar or heavy bowl. Add the pine nuts and work with a pestle or crushing tool until a smooth paste is obtained.

3 Add the egg yolk and season with the garlic, chilli powder, salt and pepper. Transfer to a bowl and progressively whisk in the olive oil until a thick mayonnaise is formed.

4 Heat 2 tbsp olive oil and cook the fillets (skin side down first) for 3-5 minutes, turning a couple of times.

5 Serve the fillets warm or cold with the mayonnaise. Sprinkle over the chopped chives just before serving.

Right: **From eastern waters, a recipe for Red Mullet with Mayonnaise.**

TROUT FILLETS WITH HERBS

Here, marinated trout with crispy herb shells are accompanied with buttered spinach.

INGREDIENTS

4 trout, cut into fillets

6 tbsp olive oil

Juice of 1 lemon

1 clove garlic, finely chopped

2 tbsp chopped fresh herbs

5 tbsp fresh breadcrumbs

1 tbsp oil melted with 1 tbsp nut butter

2 cups spinach leaves, washed, dried and chopped

1 tbsp butter

175 ml/6 fl oz fish stock

6 tbsp single cream

2 tbsp chopped tomato

SERVES: 4

TIME: Preparation takes about 30 minutes, plus marinating time of 1 hour. Cooking takes approximately 40 minutes.

1 Mix the 6 tbsp oil with the lemon juice and marinate the fillets in the mixture for 1 hour.

2 Mix together the garlic, herbs and breadcrumbs. Drain the fillets and toss them in the herbed breadcrumbs.

3 Heat the oil and butter in a frying pan. Add the fillets and cook them gently, skin side first, then turn the fillets over, raise the heat and crisp up the other side. Allow to reach a nice golden-brown colour.

4 Meanwhile, sauté the spinach leaves in the butter, taking care not to overcook.

5 Place the stock in a saucepan, boil to reduce by half, remove from the heat and stir in the cream. Blend the sauce in a blender until smooth.

6 Serve the spinach next to the crisp fillets, with the sauce poured around the spinach and the tomato dotted over.

MARINATED SARDINES

This recipe comes from Spain. The sardines are usually served with fresh, crusty bread.

INGREDIENTS

10 sardines

1 red pepper

3 tbsp olive oil

Salt and pepper

2 shallots, finely chopped

225 ml/8 fl oz vinegar or wine
  vinegar

SERVES: 4

1 Remove the central bone from the sardines and separate the fillets in two.

2 Prepare the pepper by dicing it quite finely.

3 Heat the olive oil and sear the fillets quickly on each side for approximately 15 seconds, then drain on kitchen paper. Season with salt and pepper.

4 In the same oil, sauté the shallots and pepper but do not allow them to brown.

5 Deglaze the pan with the vinegar and allow to reduce for 30 seconds.

6 Remove from the heat and pour all the ingredients over the fish in a shallow serving dish. Put in the refrigerator to marinate for 24 hours. Bring back to room temperature before serving.

TIME: Preparation takes 30 minutes, cooking takes about 5 minutes and 24 hours for marinating.

PIZZA WITH MIXED SEAFOOD

INGREDIENTS

TOMATO SAUCE:

1 tbsp olive oil
½ small onion
1 clove garlic, crushed
340 g/12 oz chopped
    tomatoes
Chopped fresh herbs
    (optional)

23 cm/9-inch pizza base
60 g/2 oz tin anchovy fillets,
    drained
175 g/ 6 oz mixed seafood e.g.
    prawns, mussels, squid, etc.
2 tsp capers
55 g/2 oz Bel Paese cheese
55 g/2 oz full-fat cream cheese

SERVES: 2-4

TIME: Preparation takes about
30 minutes and cooking takes
about 15 minutes.

1 Heat the oil in a saucepan, add the
onion and fry until beginning to soften.
Add the garlic and cook for 1 minute.
Add the tomatoes and bring slowly to
the boil. Stir in the herbs, reduce the
heat and simmer for 20 minutes.

2 Spread the tomato sauce over the
pizza base and arrange the anchovies
on top. Spread the seafood over the
anchovies and sprinkle with the capers.

3 Beat together the two cheeses and
place blobs of the mixture over the
pizza. Bake in a preheated 180°C/
350°F/gas mark 4 oven for 12-15
minutes, or until the cheese has melted.

Cook's tip: The packs of frozen
mixed seafood available in many
supermarkets make this recipe very
easy to prepare.

*Top left: **Marinated Sardines**.*
*Left: **Pizza with Mixed Seafood**.*
*Opposite page: **A panoramic view of
an anchorage in Turkey with its
crystal-clear waters**.*

SCAMPI WITH GARLIC

This Spanish dish of fresh scampi sautéed with garlic and wine is simply prepared yet delicious.

INGREDIENTS

16 fresh scampi or large
  prawns

4 garlic cloves

3 tbsp olive oil

Salt and pepper

1 tbsp sherry vinegar

115 ml/4 fl oz sweet white
  wine

2 tomatoes, seeded and cut
  into small cubes

Chopped chives

SERVES: 4

TIME: Preparation takes about
25 minutes and cooking takes
approximately 5 minutes.

Above right: **The fishing fleet has returned and trays of fish glisten, their aroma the test of freshness.**

1 Remove the shells and prepare the scampi, cutting away the heads and shells. Run the tip of a sharp knife down the back of each and remove the black vein which runs down it.

2 Cut the cloves of garlic into very thin slices. Heat the olive oil in a frying pan and add the garlic. Allow to colour to a golden brown. Add the scampi and season with salt and pepper.

3 Fry the scampi evenly. Deglaze the pan with the vinegar and wine. Allow to reduce until the liquid is almost evaporated, turning the scampi from time to time.

4 Serve hot with the tomato and chives sprinkled over.

Cook's tip: If you are sure that the scampi are very fresh, sauté them for just a few minutes. Guests can then appreciate the cooked and slightly raw flavours together.

Freezer tip: Frozen scampi are usually of very good quality. Defrost them completely and pat dry with kitchen paper.

Checkpoint: Remove the green central shoot from the garlic cloves to make them more digestible.

BOW-TIE SOLE IN OYSTER SAUCE

INGREDIENTS

3 sole fillets

225 g/8 oz mushrooms, rinsed, wiped and finely sliced

2 tomatoes, wiped and diced

440 ml/16 fl oz fish stock

3 tbsp double cream

Salt and pepper

12 oysters, shells removed

SERVES: 6

1 Cut the sole fillets lengthways into two and tie each piece into a knot. This makes the 'bow tie'.

2 Cook the mushrooms and half of the tomatoes in the stock for 5 minutes. Add the 'bow ties' and cook gently for about 5 minutes.

3 Remove the fillets with a slotted spoon. Remove the sauce from the heat and stir in the cream and seasoning.

4 Arrange the 'bow ties' neatly on a preheated serving dish.

5 Blend the sauce with a hand mixer until smooth. Stir the oysters into the sauce and allow to stand for a minute to allow them to heat through. Pour the sauce over the 'bow ties', sprinkle over the remaining diced tomato and serve immediately.

TIME: Preparation takes 10 minutes and cooking takes 30 minutes in total.

Right: **Bow-tie Sole in Oyster Sauce provides an imaginative way of serving this seafood.**

EEL IN RED WINE

INGREDIENTS

550 g/1¼ lb eel, skinned

Salt and pepper

2 tbsp olive oil

2 onions, finely sliced

1 clove garlic, chopped

300 ml/11 fl oz red wine

1 tsp sugar

3 tbsp chopped tomato

115 ml/4 fl oz fish stock

1 Cut the eel into medium-thick slices and season with salt and pepper.

2 Heat the oil and fry the onion and garlic for 1 minute. Add the eel slices to the pan and seal on both sides.

3 Stir the wine and sugar into the pan, cook until the wine reduces somewhat, then add the tomato and the fish stock. Season with salt and pepper.

4 Transfer to an ovenproof dish and

cook in a preheated 180°C/350°F/gas mark 4 oven for 15 minutes.

5 Remove the eel from the dish and, if the sauce is not very thick, pour it into a saucepan and thicken and reduce it over a high heat. Serve the eel hot, with the sauce poured over.

SERVES: 4

TIME: Preparation takes about 20 minutes and cooking takes 25 minutes.

WHELK AND COCKLE SALAD

In this Italian dish, whelks and cockles are served on a bed of tossed salad.

INGREDIENTS

32 large whelks

300 g/11 oz cockles

1 carrot, sliced

1 leek, sliced

1 onion, sliced

175 ml/6 fl oz white wine

1 sprig thyme

1 bay leaf

Small bunch chives

Juice of 1 lemon

55 ml/2 fl oz olive oil

Salt and pepper

4 small servings of mixed
  lettuce leaves, washed
  and dried

SERVES: 4

TIME: Preparation takes about
40 minutes, cooling about
30 minutes and cooking
approximately 2 hours.

1 Wash the shellfish well in cold water. Brush with a small nailbrush to remove any sand or grit. Rinse under cold, running water.

2 Place the whelks in a saucepan of water with the carrot, leek and onion. Bring to the boil and then simmer gently for approximately 2 hours, or until they are cooked. Cooking time will depend on the size of the whelks.

3 Place the cockles in a frying pan with the white wine, thyme and bay leaf. Cover, bring the contents to a brisk boil and cook until the shells open.

4 Remove from the heat when the shells are opened and allow to cool. Once they are cool enough to handle, remove the cockles from their shells and discard everything else.

5 When the whelks are cooked, set them aside to cool and then remove them from their shells. Pull off any black parts from the body of the whelk and

also the muscle at the bottom of the body. The intestinal tract may also be removed, if desired.

6 Chop the chives finely and stir them into the lemon juice, olive oil, salt and pepper. Toss the prepared lettuce, whelks and cockles in the sauce and serve on individual plates.

MUSSEL RISOTTO

This simple Italian risotto is fit for even the most sophisticated dinner party.

INGREDIENTS

1.2 litres/2 pints small mussels

1 shallot, chopped

115 ml/4 fl oz white wine

55 g/2 oz butter

1 onion, chopped

460 g/1 lb rice

Saffron

Salt and pepper

SERVES: 4

TIME: Preparation takes about 10 minutes and total cooking time is approximately 35 minutes.

Watchpoint: Do not add too much salt to the dish as the mussels provide a salty flavour of their own.

Above left: **The impressive Furore Valley on Italy's Amalfi Coast.**
Left: **Mussel Risotto.**

1 Clean the mussels under plenty of running water, scraping and brushing off any sand and grit. Place the clean mussels in a large saucepan with the shallot and the wine and cook over high heat until the mussels open. Discard any mussels that do not open.

2 Set the saucepan aside to allow the mussels to cool, then remove the mussels from their shells. Strain the cooking juices through a fine sieve which has been covered with muslin. Discard all but the juice and the mussels.

3 Melt the butter in a frying pan and gently fry the onion and rice until the rice is transparent (approximately 1 minute). Pour over the cooking juices made up to 750 ml/26 fl oz with water. Stir in 2-3 pinches of saffron – just enough to slightly colour the liquid.

4 Transfer to an ovenproof dish, season and stir in the mussels. Cover and cook in a preheated 200°C/400°F/gas mark 6 oven for about 20 minutes. Serve hot.

SCALLOPS WITH PARSLEY AND GARLIC

INGREDIENTS

20 scallops, rinsed

Salt and pepper

Flour for coating

30 g/1 oz butter

2 tsp chopped garlic

2 tsp chopped parsley

SERVES: 4

1 Dry the scallops well and season them. Toss the scallops in the flour, shaking off any excess.

2 Melt the butter in a frying pan, add the scallops and sear over high heat. Reduce the heat, add the garlic and parsley and cook for a minute or two, stirring the scallops often. Serve hot.

TIME: Preparation takes 20 minutes and cooking takes 15 minutes.

MARINATED TUNA FISH

INGREDIENTS

1 large slice tuna fish

2 tbsp butter

1 onion, finely chopped

1 tbsp chopped parsley

10 coriander seeds, crushed

1 tsp chopped garlic

Juice of 1 lemon

Cumin

Salt and pepper

2 tbsp olive oil

SERVES: 2-4

1 Place the tuna on an ovenproof plate, spread over the butter and sprinkle with the onion, parsley, coriander seeds, garlic and lemon juice. Season with a little cumin, salt and pepper.

2 Pour over the olive oil and marinate in the refrigerator for at least 2 hours.

3 Place the fish and marinade in a preheated 200°C/400°F/gas mark 6 oven and cook for 20 minutes.

4 When the fish is cooked, remove the skin and pull out the bones. Serve the fish hot with the marinade.

Serving idea: Serve with a tossed green salad or fresh green beans.

TIME: Preparation takes 20 minutes, marinating 2 hours and cooking 20 minutes.

STUFFED SQUID

An Italian fish stuffing enlivens the squid in this tasty recipe.

INGREDIENTS

8 medium squid

225 g/8 oz whitefish fillet, (cod or whiting)

2 tbsp double cream

Pinch saffron

2 tbsp chopped chives

½ egg, beaten

Salt and pepper

115 g/4 oz butter

1 tsp chopped garlic

1 tbsp chopped parsley

SERVES: 4

TIME: Preparation takes about 45 minutes and cooking takes 20 minutes.

Above left: **Stuffed Squid.**
Left: **Marinated Tuna Fish** *from Morocco, whose northern coast is visited by Atlantic bluefin tuna.*

1 Skin and clean out the squid. Rinse and dry the inside very carefully.

2 Place the fish fillets in a food processor, with the double cream, saffron, chives and the ½ egg. Season with salt and pepper, and process until smooth. Chill.

3 Place the stuffing in a pastry bag with a plain nozzle. Stuff each squid three-quarters full, pushing the stuffing in lightly. Sew up the end of each squid using a needle and thick thread.

4 Melt the butter in a frying pan and fry the stuffed squid evenly. Transfer to an ovenproof dish, add the garlic and parsley, and bake in a preheated 180°C/350°F/gas mark 4 oven until cooked through – about 20 minutes.

5 Serve whole, or cut into slices with the cooking liquid.

Cook's tip: Do not overfill the squid as they tend to shrink during cooking.

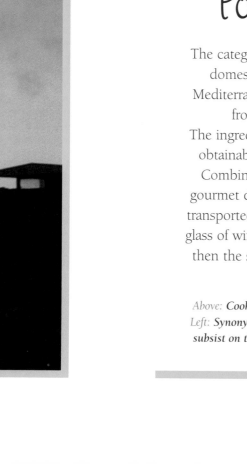

Poultry and Game

The category 'poultry and game' includes a great variety of domestically raised and wild species, but among the Mediterranean countries some favourite dishes are created from chicken, duck, quail, rabbit and turkey.
The ingredients may be simple, but that makes them easily obtainable, and the resulting recipes are a sheer delight.
Combining common elements in new ways to produce gourmet dishes is a kind of alchemy. In an instant, you are transported to a restaurant overlooking the Mediterranean – glass of wine in hand, a fine meal served at your table – and then the sun casts its rays to transmute the scene to gold.

*Above: **Cooked right in front of you, freshness and flavour are assured.***
*Left: **Synonymous with the North African desert, the Arabian camel can subsist on thorny plants, dry grasses and infrequent supplies of water.***

SADDLE OF RABBIT

Saddle of rabbit is served with Swiss chard and wild mushrooms in this elaborate Spanish recipe.

INGREDIENTS

2 large rabbit saddles (backs)

Salt and pepper

2 tbsp chopped olives

3 tbsp currants

1 large stick Swiss chard
(green part removed and
discarded)

4 tbsp olive oil

1 tsp finely chopped garlic

1 tsp finely chopped parsley

55 g/2 oz butter

4 tbsp small wild mushrooms,
washed and trimmed

SERVES: 4

TIME: Preparation takes approximately 1 hour and 30 minutes. Cooking takes about 45 minutes.

1 Bone the rabbit saddles one by one. Begin by slicing into the underside of the saddle, using a very sharp knife. Little by little, cut under the flesh and over the first bones, easing back the meat as you go along. Cut the meat off the carcass. Repeat on each side of the two saddles.

2 Season the boned meat fillets with salt and pepper and sprinkle over the chopped olives. Roll up the meat and secure tightly with string. Set aside.

3 To make a rich rabbit stock, break up the carcasses a little and fry them in 1 tbsp oil. Add 1 tbsp currants, cover with water, and boil until reduced to a quite thick stock.

4 Cut the Swiss chard into very small cubes and sauté in 1 tbsp oil with half of the garlic, half the parsley and the remaining currants. Set aside when cooked.

5 Sauté the meat rolls in 2 tbsp oil and a little butter. Once browned, transfer to an ovenproof dish and cook in a preheated 180°C/350°F/gas mark 4 oven for 25 minutes.

6 Sauté the mushrooms in the remaining butter with the remaining garlic and parsley. Season with salt and pepper. Set aside.

7 Strain the stock through a very fine sieve. Return to a high heat to reduce and thicken. If desired, whip in the remaining butter and blend smooth with a hand mixer. Adjust seasoning, adding salt and pepper as necessary.

8 Cut the meat into rounds. Accompany with the reheated Swiss chard, the mushrooms and the sauce.

Buying guide: If preferred, use the boned rabbit meat now available in many supermarkets.

Cook's tip: Keep your knife as close to the bones as possible, so as not to lose any meat.

LAPIN CHASSEUR

'Hunter's rabbit' is a delicious blend of mushrooms, smoked bacon and white wine.

INGREDIENTS

1 rabbit

115 g/¼ lb smoked bacon, diced

1 onion, chopped

220 ml/8 fl oz white wine

1 bouquet garni

Pinch nutmeg

Salt and pepper

340 g/12 oz button mushrooms, sliced

1 tbsp butter

1 tbsp flour

1 tbsp chopped parsley

SERVES: 4-6

TIME: Preparation takes about 15 minutes and cooking takes approximately 45 minutes.

1 Bone the rabbit and cut the meat into small pieces.

2 Cook the bacon in a casserole on the top of the cooker, without adding any extra fat, until the fat runs from the bacon. Stir in the rabbit pieces, add the onion and continue cooking until the onion is tender.

3 Pour over the wine and 250 ml/9 fl oz water. Add the bouquet garni, nutmeg, salt and pepper. Bring to the boil. Cover, reduce the heat and cook for 30 minutes.

4 Add the mushrooms and simmer gently for a further 15 minutes.

5 Just before serving, beat together the butter and the flour. Beat this into the sauce, off the heat, little by little until the sauce thickens to the desired consistency. Serve with the parsley sprinkled over.

QUAIL IN FILO PASTRY

Filo pastry is stuffed with quail meat, fresh figs and almonds in this unusual recipe.

INGREDIENTS

4 quail, cleaned and singed

2 handfuls wild mushrooms (ceps and girolles)

4 tbsp olive oil

1 tbsp chopped almonds

Salt and pepper

4 sheets filo pastry

4 fresh figs, cubed

2 tbsp melted butter

SERVES: 4

TIME: Preparation takes about 30 minutes and cooking takes 10-15 minutes.

Above left: **Quail in Filo Pastry** *from Tunisia captures the flavour of wild mushrooms, figs and almonds.*
Lower left: **Lapin Chasseur**, *or* **Hunter's Rabbit**, *makes a tasty meal at the end of a busy day.*

1 Remove the legs and wings from the quails and cut the meat off them.

2 Cut off and discard any stems from the mushrooms. Cut the caps into small pieces and wash them well. Set aside to drain.

3 Heat 2 tbsp oil and fry the mushrooms with the almonds for 2 minutes. Season with salt and pepper and set aside.

4 Gently fry the quail breasts and legs in 1 tbsp oil for 1 minute. Set the legs aside and cut the breast meat into thin slices.

5 Spread out the filo sheets and brush them all over with the melted butter.

6 Place a little of the mushroom mixture and the sliced breast meat in the centre of each sheet. Season with a little salt and pepper.

7 Sprinkle the cubed figs around the mushrooms and meat, still keeping everything in the centre. Fold over the ends and then the sides, working to form a small rectangular shape.

8 Heat the remaining oil and fry the packets evenly. Transfer to an ovenproof dish and cook in a preheated 200°C/400°F/gas mark 6 oven for 5 minutes, along with the legs.

9 Serve the packets hot, with the quail legs and any remaining mushrooms slightly reheated.

Serving idea: Serve with a lettuce leaf salad tossed in vinegar and almond oil dressing.

Variation: If fresh figs are not in season, use dried figs, apricots or dates.

Checkpoint: The packets are just sealed for a minute or two in the hot oil and transferred to the oven. Be careful that they do not overbrown.

CHICKEN WITH ALMONDS

A delicious Spanish dish which incorporates boned chicken meat in a rich nut cream sauce.

INGREDIENTS

1 chicken

115 g/4 oz blanched almonds

115 g/4 oz shelled walnuts

55 g/2 oz butter

600 ml/1 pint chicken stock

Salt and pepper

4 tbsp double cream

2 tbsp olive oil

4 slices white bread, cubed
    and fried (optional)

SERVES: 4

TIME: **Preparation takes about
45 minutes and cooking takes
approximately 30 minutes.**

Checkpoint: When you
add the stock to the pan in
step 4, there should be
enough liquid to cover the
chicken meat.

Right: **A typical colourful street
scene in Spain.**

1 Bone the chicken and cut the meat into even slices.

2 If using fresh shelled almonds, blanch them by soaking in boiling water for a few minutes. Drain and rinse them under cold water. Squeeze each almond between thumb and forefinger to ease off the skin.

3 Grind the almonds and walnuts together in a food processor (not too finely).

4 Melt the butter and gently cook the sliced chicken for 2 minutes. Do not allow the meat to brown. Remove the meat and add the ground nut mixture. Stir-fry for 2 minutes, pour over the stock and return the sliced chicken to the pan. Season with salt and pepper.

5 Cook over a gentle heat for 20 minutes. Remove the chicken with a slotted spoon and keep warm. Return the pan to a high heat to reduce. Whip in the cream and bring to the boil again.

6 Reduce the heat and return the chicken to the pan. Do not allow the sauce to reboil. Serve the chicken garnished with croutons, if you wish.

Variation: Try a mixture of cashews and hazelnuts instead of walnuts and almonds, or try other nut blends.

RICE-STUFFED CHICKEN BREASTS

A light Algerian entrée of chicken breast stuffed with raisins and rice in a butter sauce.

INGREDIENTS

½ onion, chopped

2 tbsp raisins

4 tbsp olive oil

115 g/4 oz rice

1.2 litres/2 pints chicken stock

Nutmeg

Salt and pepper

4 chicken breasts

1 egg, beaten

55g/2 oz butter

SERVES: 4

TIME: Preparation takes about 40 minutes and cooking takes approximately 1 hour.

1 Gently fry the onions and raisins in 2 tbsp oil. Add the rice and, stirring continuously, cook until the rice becomes transparent (1 minute). Pour over 900 ml/1½ pints chicken stock and season with nutmeg, salt and pepper. Cover and cook in a preheated 200°C/400°F/gas mark 6 oven for 20 minutes.

2 Cut the chicken breasts open (do not cut them in two) to form a 'pocket'. Season the breasts inside and out and fill the pockets with a little of the cooked rice. Push down slightly.

3 Brush the edges of the bottom slice with beaten egg and then press down to 'seal' with the upper part of the breast.

4 Sauté the chicken breasts on both sides in the remaining oil. Pour over the remaining stock, cover and cook on a moderate heat for 25 minutes.

5 Remove the cooked breasts, allow the stock to reduce over a high heat and whisk in the butter, a small piece at a

time. Check the seasoning. Serve the breasts with the remaining rice and the sauce.

Variation: For those watching their weight, reduce calories by steaming the stuffed breasts and serving with the reduced stock (without the butter).

WALNUT RABBIT

This delicious Italian concoction combines walnuts, olives and white wine.

INGREDIENTS

1 rabbit, boned and the meat cut into small pieces

2 tbsp olive oil

1 onion, finely chopped

1 small stick celery, finely chopped

15 green olives, stoned and finely chopped

15 walnuts, shelled

520 ml/18 fl oz white wine

520 ml/18 fl oz chicken stock

Salt and pepper

½ tsp mustard

2 tbsp double cream

SERVES: 4

TIME: Preparation takes about 25 minutes and cooking takes approximately 1 hour and 30 minutes.

1 Heat the oil in a flameproof casserole and gently fry the onion and celery until tender.

2 Add the rabbit meat, stir, and add the olives and walnuts. Cook for 5 minutes, stirring frequently. Pour in the wine and cook over a high heat until the wine has almost evaporated.

3 Pour over the stock and add a little water to cover. Season with salt and pepper and cook on a low heat until the rabbit is tender and the juices somewhat reduced.

4 Remove the meat and whisk in the mustard and cream; do not let the sauce boil. Replace the meat, stir and serve.

DUCK IN ORANGE SAUCE

*A great classic, duck has always been very popular
in France, and wild duck is much sought after.*

INGREDIENTS

1 large duck, prepared, dried
and cut into pieces

8 oranges, washed and dried

1 carrot, scraped and
shredded

1 onion, finely chopped

30 g/1 oz butter

1 tbsp vinegar

1 tbsp cornflour, dissolved
in 1 tbsp water

Salt and pepper

SERVES: 6

TIME: Preparation takes
50 minutes and cooking
takes about 1 hour.

1 Peel the skin from 2 of the oranges
with a potato peeler and cut it into fine
strips. Blanch the strips in boiling water
for a few minutes, drain well and set
aside. Retain the oranges for the juice.

2 Peel 4 more oranges and cut the flesh
into thick slices.

3 Melt half the butter in a heavy
saucepan and brown the duck pieces
on all sides. Reduce the heat, add the
carrot, onion and 2 tbsp water.
Cover and cook for about 30 minutes,
turning the duck pieces from time to
time. Add a little water if necessary
during cooking.

4 Remove the duck pieces from the
pan and wrap up tightly in aluminium
foil. Strain the juices from the pan
through a fine sieve and pour into a
clean saucepan.

5 Squeeze the juice of the peeled
oranges and the remaining 2 oranges.
Add this to the strained juices and stir

well. Add the vinegar and the orange
strips. Cook over a low heat for
a few minutes.

6 Stir in the dissolved cornflour, stirring
continuously until the sauce begins to
thicken. Remove from the heat and
keep warm.

7 Cut the meat off the duck and place
it on a serving dish.

8 In a clean saucepan, cook the orange
slices in the remaining butter until they
have taken on a little colour. Add the
sauce, stir, and serve poured over the
duck pieces.

Watchpoint: When peeling the
oranges, be careful not to include any
white pith as this will give the dish a
bitter flavour.

SLICED CHICKEN WITH FIGS

A new recipe that presents chicken in a fresh light ~ this will delight all who taste it.

INGREDIENTS

1 large chicken, boned and
   cut into slices

30 g/1 oz butter

1 tbsp oil

1 small stick cinnamon

220 ml/8 fl oz white wine

220 ml/8 fl oz chicken stock

Pinch saffron

15 coriander seeds

6 dried figs, each cut into 3

2 tsp honey

Salt and pepper

SERVES: 6

TIME: Preparation takes about
5 minutes and cooking takes
about 35 minutes.

Above left: **Duck in Orange Sauce is
a long-time favourite in France.**
Left: **Sliced Chicken with Figs is an
innovative Gallic recipe.**

1 In a heavy frying pan, melt the butter
and the oil and fry the chicken slices.
Allow to brown slightly, then remove from
the heat.

2 Remove the chicken from the frying
pan and keep it warm. Put the frying pan
back on the heat and add the cinnamon
stick, wine, stock, saffron, coriander seeds,
figs, honey, salt and pepper. Stir well and
cook for 4 minutes. Return the chicken to
the frying pan, cover, and cook for
20 minutes on a very gentle heat.

3 Remove the chicken and the figs and
keep them warm. Remove and discard the
cinnamon stick.

4 Allow the sauce to boil until quite
syrupy. Return the chicken and figs to the
frying pan, heat through and serve.

Watchpoint: Cook over a very gentle
heat throughout step 2, stirring from time
to time to prevent sticking.

QUAIL SALAD

This Italian recipe features quail meat served on a green salad with cubes of fried bread and a delicious sauce.

INGREDIENTS

4 fresh quail

5 tbsp vegetable oil

½ carrot, chopped

1 shallot, chopped

Salt and pepper

1 tbsp olive oil

Vinegar

4 slices of white bread

4 servings of mixed green salad

SERVES: 4

TIME: Preparation takes about 10 minutes and total cooking time is approximately 40 minutes.

1 Remove the legs and the breast meat from the quail. Draw the birds if this has not been done by the butcher.

2 Heat 1 tbsp vegetable oil in a pan and add the wings and carcasses. Brown well and cover with 300 ml/½ pint water. Add the carrot and shallot, and season with salt and pepper. Leave on a high heat until the stock has reduced by half. Strain the stock through a fine sieve and discard the bones.

3 Put the stock back on a high heat and cook until it becomes quite syrupy. Remove from the heat, allow to cool, then stir in the olive oil and a drop of vinegar. Stir well and set aside.

4 Cut the sliced bread into small cubes. Heat 2 tbsp oil in a frying pan and fry the cubes on all sides. Drain on kitchen paper when golden.

5 Season the quail meat and legs with lots of salt and pepper, and sauté in the remaining oil until cooked through

completely. Serve the legs and quail meat on a bed of salad with the sauce poured over.

Cook's tip: When cooking the quail breasts in the oil, begin skin-side down and turn often to prevent the meat from drying out.

CHICKEN AND LEMON TAGINE

Chicken is combined with lemon, spices and herbs in this aromatic recipe.

INGREDIENTS

1 chicken
2 saumure lemons
1 tbsp chopped parsley
1 tbsp chopped coriander
Pinch cinnamon
Pinch cumin
Pinch saffron
Salt and pepper
10 coriander seeds
1 onion, chopped
175 ml/6 fl oz olive oil
340 ml/12 fl oz water

SERVES: 4

TIME: Preparation takes about 25 minutes, marinating takes 1 hour and cooking takes about 1 hour 30 minutes.

Serving idea: Cooked semolina, with a few raisins sprinkled over, is an ideal accompaniment.

1 Bone the chicken and cut the meat into small pieces.

2 Cut the lemons into quarters and place them with the herbs in a bowl. Sprinkle over the cinnamon, cumin, saffron, salt, pepper and coriander seeds. Add the onion and olive oil to make a marinade.

3 Add the chicken and marinate for 1 hour in a cool place.

4 Place the chicken and marinade in an ovenproof dish or tagine pot. Add the water, cover and cook in a preheated 160°C/325°F/gas mark 3 oven for 1 hour and 30 minutes or until the chicken is cooked. Check the dish from time to time, adding more water if necessary.

Buying guide: Saumure lemons are whole lemons pickled in vinegar and salt. Substitute 1 ordinary lemon if saumure lemons are unavailable.

QUAIL WITH GRAPES

Quail is becoming increasingly available and provides the perfect answer when an impressive meal is required.

INGREDIENTS

6 quail

115 g/4 oz butter

2 tbsp oil

120 ml/4 fl oz Madeira

340 g/¾ lb seedless white grapes

440 ml/16 fl oz chicken stock

Salt and pepper

6 slices white bread

SERVES: 6

TIME: Preparation takes about 20 minutes and cooking takes approximately 40 minutes.

1 To prepare the birds, remove the heads and wings, then draw the quail and truss them with kitchen string.

2 Melt a knob of the butter and 1 tbsp oil in a frying pan and gently brown the birds. Remove from the pan and finish cooking in a preheated 200°C/400°F/ gas mark 6 oven for about 15 minutes.

3 Pour off any excess fat from the pan and deglaze the pan with the Madeira. Add the grapes and then stir in the stock. Allow to reduce to a syrupy consistency.

4 Remove the grapes using a slotted spoon. Whip the remaining butter, reserving a knob for the toasts, and season with salt and pepper. Blend smooth with a hand mixer and replace the grapes.

5 Fry the bread in the knob of butter with the remaining oil. Serve the quail on the toasts, with the sauce poured over the top.

Cook's tip: The grapes can be peeled, but the skins are necessary for the sauce, so add them at step 3 and then remove them just before serving.

Watchpoint: Drain the toasts on kitchen paper before serving to remove the excess fat.

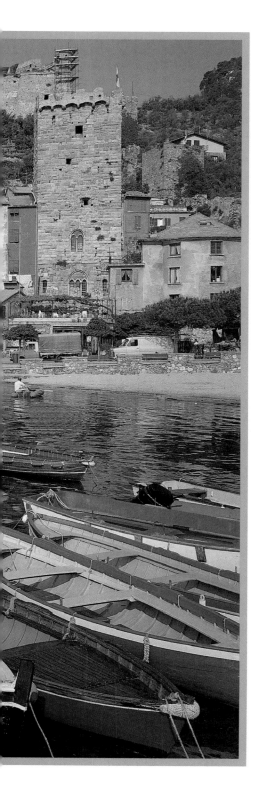

Meat Dishes

Culinary customs are developed and refined over millennia. The sun-scorched lands of the Mediterranean offer little by way of grazing for large herds of animals, so small-scale husbandry became the normal practice, with meat regarded as something of a luxury. As such, recipes evolved to make the most of any meat, with other ingredients – such as onions, rice, nuts, potatoes and vegetables – often added to the dish to make the meal go a little further. Today, of course, the standard of living is much higher in the region, but the traditional ways of preparing meat dishes are still retained and the results are simply exquisite.

Above: **Strings of sausages for sale in Turkey.**
Left: **Dominated by the 12th-16th century citadel, the harbour at Portovenere, Italy, is lined with bars and restaurants.**

Lamb with Mint Tagine

From Morocco, this recipe is a flavourful way to cook lamb, especially for those who like the unusual.

Ingredients

460 g/1 lb lamb (shoulder)

280 ml/10 fl oz olive oil

340 ml/12 fl oz water

1 onion, chopped

1 tbsp honey

1 tbsp chopped coriander

20 mint leaves

Ras el hanout (ground cloves, cinnamon and black pepper, mixed)

1 tsp hot pepper paste (*harissa*)

Salt

Serves: 4

Time: Preparation takes about 20 minutes and cooking takes 1 hour and 30 minutes.

Serving idea: Ratatouille makes a good vegetable accompaniment.

Variation: Shoulder meat can be replaced with leg of lamb or even neck.

1 Cut the meat into small cubes. Place the meat and olive oil in an ovenproof dish or tagine, and cover with water.

2 Add the onion and stir in the honey, coriander, mint, *ras el hanout* to taste, hot pepper paste and salt.

3 Cover and cook in a preheated 150°C/300°F/gas mark 2 oven for 1 hour and 30 minutes. Serve very hot as soon as the meat is cooked.

Variation: If you cannot buy fresh mint, use dried.

Above: **The distinctive, tall lateen rig of an Egyptian felucca.**
Left: **Lamb with Mint Tagine.**

MOUSSAKA

This famous Greek classic has baked layers of aubergine, minced lamb, onion and bechamel sauce, topped with cheese.

INGREDIENTS

BECHAMEL:

2 tbsp butter

2 tbsp flour

280 ml/10 fl oz milk

Salt and pepper

Pinch nutmeg

3 aubergines, cut into even-sized slices

Little flour for coating

5 tbsp olive oil

Salt and pepper

1 onion, chopped

340 g/12 oz minced lamb

4 tbsp grated cheese (Cheddar or similar)

1 Melt the butter in a saucepan, stir the flour into the butter and heat the mixture gently for 1 minute.

2 Gradually add the milk. Stir and cook until thickened. Remove from the heat and season with the nutmeg, salt and pepper. Stir well and set aside.

3 Coat the aubergine slices with a little flour. Heat the olive oil and fry the slices on both sides. Drain on kitchen paper. Season with salt and pepper.

Right: **The classic Greek dish, Moussaka.**

4 Mix together the onion and the minced meat.

5 Grease an ovenproof dish. Cover the bottom with a layer of aubergine slices. Add a layer of meat, then a layer of bechamel sauce. Continue until all the ingredients are used up, ending with a layer of bechamel. Cook in a preheated 190°C/375°F/gas mark 5 oven for 30-40 minutes.

6 After about 20 minutes cooking time, sprinkle with the grated cheese. Return to the oven to finish cooking.

Serving idea: Tomato sauce is a traditional accompaniment to this dish.

SERVES: 4

TIME: Preparation takes about 45 minutes and cooking time is 30-40 minutes.

KEFTA

INGREDIENTS

550 g/1¼ lb lamb (shoulder)
1 tbsp each chopped coriander
and mint
Ras el hanout (ground cloves,
cinnamon and black pepper,
mixed) to taste
Salt and pepper
1 egg
1 shallot, chopped

SERVES: 4

1 Chop the meat in a food processor, and mix in the coriander and mint. Turn the mixture into a bowl and add the *ras el hanout* and seasoning. Add the egg and shallot and mix well.

2 Dampen your fingers with water and shape the mixture into 'logs'.

3 Cook the kefta under a medium grill for about 6 minutes each side, until cooked through.

Variation: Any cut of lamb can be used for these kefta.

TIME: Preparation takes 25 minutes and cooking time is 20 minutes.

Right: **Kefta from Morocco. This rugged land has the highest mountains in North Africa covering over a third of the country.**

LAMB KEBABS

INGREDIENTS

225 g/8 oz leg of lamb
225 g/8 oz lamb's heart
225 g/8 oz lamb's kidney
1 tbsp lemon juice
Salt
Cumin
Ras el hanout (ground cloves,
cinnamon and black
pepper, mixed)
1 tsp hot pepper paste (*harissa*)
3 tbsp olive oil

1 Cut all the meat into bite-sized chunks. Push them onto skewers beginning with the lamb, followed by a piece of kidney and then a piece of heart. Continue until skewers are full.

2 Mix together the lemon juice, a few pinches of salt, a few pinches of cumin, the *ras el hanout* to taste, hot pepper paste and finally the olive oil.

3 Lay the skewers on a plate and pour over the marinade. Leave the kebabs to marinate for 12 hours or more, turning them over from time to time.

4 Cook under a medium grill for about 6 minutes each side until cooked through.

SERVES: 4

TIME: Preparation takes 20 minutes, plus one day marinating. Cooking takes about 15 minutes.

RICE BALLS

These Italian meat, cheese and rice balls are a great favourite with children and adults alike.

INGREDIENTS

200 g/7 oz cooked arborio rice

115 g/4 oz minced beef

3 slices mozzarella cheese, cubed

55 g/2 oz grated Parmesan cheese

1 tsp chopped parsley

Salt and pepper

1 egg, beaten

Breadcrumbs

Oil for deep frying

SERVES: 4

TIME: Preparation takes about 35 minutes in total. Cooking takes about 10-15 minutes.

1 Mix together the rice and minced meat. Stir in the cubed mozzarella, grated Parmesan and parsley.

2 Season well with salt and pepper, and bind together using half the beaten egg.

3 With slightly moist fingers, shape the mixture into small balls.

4 Dip the rice balls in the remaining egg and then roll in breadcrumbs. Set the balls aside to rest for 20 minutes.

5 Heat the oil to 150°C/300°F, lower in the rice balls and cook until golden and crisp. Drain on kitchen paper and serve immediately.

BLANQUETTE DE VEAU

In this recipe, cubes of veal are served in a smooth sauce.
Blanquette indicates a sauce made from a roux.

INGREDIENTS

460 g/1 lb veal, cubed

2 onions, chopped

2 carrots, chopped

1 leek, chopped

Salt and pepper

2 tbsp butter

30 g/1 oz plain flour

175 g/6 oz button mushrooms, sliced

180 ml/6 fl oz milk

180 ml/6 fl oz single cream

1 egg yolk, beaten

SERVES: 4

TIME: **Preparation takes about 10 minutes and cooking takes approximately 45 minutes.**

1 Put the cubes of meat into a heavy saucepan, cover with cold water and bring to the boil. Add the onions, carrots, leek, salt and pepper.

2 Bring to the boil once again, then reduce the heat and cover. Cook until the meat is tender, skimming off the fat that rises to the surface.

3 Remove the cooked meat and vegetables with a slotted spoon and keep warm.

4 Melt the butter in a small saucepan and stir in the flour. Stir this roux into the juices in the saucepan, adding little by little, until the sauce thickens. Add the mushrooms. Reduce the heat and cook for 15 minutes, stirring regularly.

5 Beat the milk and the cream into the egg yolk, and beat half of this mixture into the casserole. Once it is well incorporated, beat in the remaining mixture, beating continuously to avoid curdling.

6 Add the meat and vegetables, heat through and serve on a preheated serving dish.

Serving idea: This dish is traditionally served with boiled long grain rice.

LASAGNE

The classic Italian dish to serve to hungry guests, home-made lasagne may be commonplace but it is still delicious.

INGREDIENTS

2 tbsp olive oil

½ onion, chopped

1 tsp finely chopped garlic

½ red pepper, diced

460 g/1 lb minced beef

4 tomatoes, peeled, seeded and chopped

1 tbsp chopped parsley

Salt and pepper

30 g/1 oz butter

280 ml/10 fl oz beef stock

3 tbsp grated cheese (Cheddar or Parmesan)

LASAGNE DOUGH:

250 g/9 oz plain flour

2 pinches salt

2 eggs

SERVES: 4

TIME: Preparation takes about 1 hour and cooking takes about 50 minutes.

1 To make the dough, mix together the flour, salt and eggs using your hands. Bind the ingredients together into a ball. Flour the ball lightly and set aside to rest for 15 minutes.

2 Break the ball of dough into 4 pieces. Flatten out the pieces with your fingers and the palm of your hand and work them into strips.

3 Place the beginning of one of these strips in between the rollers of a pasta machine and roll through until at the end of the strip. Now take up the second strip and adhere it to the end of the first strip.

Below: **The white-domed church of Santa Maria della Salute in Venice, Italy.**

4 Continue to roll the dough through the machine, making very long, thin strips. Cut the finished strips into suitable lengths for an ovenproof dish.

5 Precook the lasagne strips in salted, boiling water for 1 minute. Drain and spread out on damp tea towels. The strips should not touch.

6 Heat the olive oil and gently sauté the onion, garlic and pepper. After 2 minutes, add the beef, tomato and parsley. Season with salt and pepper, stir well and cook until the liquid reduces. When the mixture reaches the consistency of a bolognaise sauce, remove from the heat and set aside.

7 Grease an ovenproof dish with the butter and place a layer of pasta in the bottom. Spread over a layer of meat sauce and continue layering until all the ingredients are used, ending with the sauce.

8 Pour over half of the stock and cook in a preheated 200°C/400°F/gas mark 6 oven for 30-40 minutes.

9 During cooking, add the remaining stock as necessary. Sprinkle over the grated cheese for the last 10 minutes of cooking – this should result in a crispy, golden topping. Serve hot from the oven.

LAMB MEATBALLS WITH PINE NUTS

Lamb ground with pine nuts and herbs makes wonderfully fragrant meatballs.

INGREDIENTS

460 g/1 lb lamb (shoulder)
   cut into small pieces

1 onion, chopped

1 tbsp pine nuts

1 tbsp chopped parsley

1 tbsp chopped coriander

1 tbsp chopped basil

1 egg

Salt and pepper

55 g/2 oz butter, melted

1 tbsp chopped chives

SERVES: 4

TIME: Preparation takes about 35 minutes and cooking takes approximately 20 minutes.

Above right: **Bazaars are a colourful feature of the Middle East and offer many tempting articles for sale.**
Left: **Lamb Meatballs with Pine Nuts.**

1 Place the meat in the bowl of a food processor. Add the onion, pine nuts, herbs (except the chive), egg and salt and pepper.

2 Mix everything together to form a smooth stuffing (do not process it too finely).

3 Roll small pieces of the mixture into balls between the palms of your hands and place them in an ovenproof dish.

4 Pour over the melted butter and cook in a preheated 200°C/400°F/ gas mark 6 oven for approximately 20 minutes. Shake the dish to turn the balls during cooking.

5 Serve the meatballs topped with the chopped chives.

Variation: Beef can be used in place of the lamb, although beef meatballs will not be as tender.

Cook's tip: Before rolling the meatballs, wet your hands with cold water to prevent sticking.

ROYAL COUSCOUS

This elaborate North African dish comprises kebabs, meatballs and sausages served with a spicy broth and semolina grain.

INGREDIENTS

1 carrot
1 turnip
1 onion
1 courgette
¼ cabbage
2 tomatoes
1 piece lamb (neck)
2 chicken legs
3 tbsp olive oil
¼ green chilli pepper
115 g/4 oz chickpeas
Salt and pepper
Chilli powder to taste
340 g/12 oz leg of lamb
1 egg
1 tsp chopped onion
1 tsp chopped parsley
340 g/12 oz beef fillet
1 red pepper, cubed
4 merguez (spicy sausages)
520 g/1 lb 2 oz semolina
Handful raisins
Hot pepper paste (*harissa*)

1 Cut the vegetables into large pieces and the cabbage into slices. Peel, seed and chop the tomatoes.

2 Cut the piece of lamb and the meat from the chicken legs into pieces.

3 Heat the olive oil and fry the chicken, chopped lamb and green chilli pepper evenly until lightly browned.

4 Add the chopped carrot, turnip, cabbage, onion and courgette.

5 Pour over enough water to cover. Add the chickpeas and the tomatoes. Season with salt, pepper and a little chilli powder. Cook on a gentle heat for 1 hour.

6 Meanwhile, prepare the meatballs. Process the leg of lamb with the egg and add the chopped onion and parsley. Season with salt and pepper. Form into small meatballs.

7 Make kebabs by cutting the beef into cubes and sliding them onto skewers, alternating with pieces of red pepper.

8 Cook the kebabs and merguez sausages under a hot grill. Cook the meatballs in the vegetable and lamb stock.

9 Cook the semolina according to the instructions on the packet. Stir in the raisins.

10 Remove the meatballs from the stock. Serve the semolina topped with the meats and sausages. Serve with the vegetable and meat stock. Guests can stir in a little *harissa* if they wish.

Serving idea: *Harissa* is a paste made from pounding down hot red pimento peppers. Guests should be cautioned, since it is extremely hot.

SERVES: 4

TIME: Preparation takes about 2 hours and cooking takes 1-1½ hours.

PORK FILLETS WITH PRUNES

An easy French meal to prepare and cook, with a delicious, slightly sweet sauce.

INGREDIENTS
1 kg/2¼ lb pork fillet
20 rashers smoked bacon
1 tbsp olive oil
1 shallot, finely chopped
½ carrot, finely chopped
2 tbsp port
300 ml/½ pint chicken stock
225 g/8 oz prunes
Salt and pepper

SERVES: 6

TIME: Preparation will take about 20 minutes and cooking takes approximately 40 minutes.

Freezer: The sauce can be made in advance and stored in the freezer.

Above left: **Royal Couscous from Morocco.**
Left: **Pork Fillets with Prunes.**

1 Remove any fat from the meat. Cut into small steaks, roll a strip of bacon around the outside of each steak and secure with kitchen string.

2 Heat the olive oil in a frying pan, add the steaks and seal on both sides.

3 Cook the steaks in a preheated 180°C/350°F/gas mark 4 oven for about 20 minutes. Cooking time depends on the thickness of the meat and individual taste.

4 Wipe out the excess oil from the frying pan and gently cook the shallot and carrot. Increase heat, add the port and then the stock. Bring to the boil and allow to reduce by about a third.

5 Pour the sauce into a blender and blend, adding ¾ of the pitted prunes, a few at a time, until the mixture is smooth. Return the sauce to the heat, season and warm through.

6 Serve the steaks on the sauce and garnish with the remaining whole prunes.

BEEF STUFFED WITH EGGS

This spicy minced meat loaf from Egypt is stuffed with quail eggs.

INGREDIENTS

550 g/1¼ lb minced beef

2 eggs, one beaten

1 tsp chopped parsley

½ onion, chopped

Salt and pepper

Pinch cardamom

Pinch cumin

Pinch nutmeg

10 quail eggs, hard boiled and shelled

Flour for coating

Breadcrumbs for coating

30 g/1 oz butter, melted

SERVES: 4

TIME: Preparation takes 45 minutes and resting time is 15 minutes. Cooking takes 35 minutes.

1 Mix the meat and one egg together in a food processor.

2 Season the meat with the parsley, onion, salt, pepper, cardamom, cumin and nutmeg. Mix well, then spread the meat mixture on a floured surface to form 2 rectangles.

3 Place the quail eggs down the centre of one of the rectangles. Brush a little beaten egg around the edges of the meat.

4 Place the second rectangle over the first and shape it into a large sausage-like shape. Roll the 'sausage' in flour, then in the beaten egg and then in the breadcrumbs. Repeat the operation two or three times. Place in a cool place for approximately 15 minutes.

5 Brown the meat loaf in the butter on all sides. Transfer to a preheated 180°C/ 350°F/gas mark 4 oven and bake for 35 minutes. Cut into slices and serve.

Serving idea: A spicy tomato sauce makes a good accompaniment for this dish.

Cook's tip: Flour the meat roll well, so that the meat stays in place.

*Left: **Statue of Ramses II, pharaoh of ancient Egypt and hero of a war against the Hittites.**
Right: **Beef Stuffed with Eggs.***

CARPACCIO WITH FRESH BASIL

INGREDIENTS
460 g/1 lb beef fillet
2 tbsp olive oil
2 cloves garlic, finely chopped
1 squeeze lemon juice
10 fresh basil leaves
Salt and pepper

SERVES: 4

TIME: Preparation takes 30 minutes.

1 Slice the meat thinly and spread out on a serving plate.

2 Mix together the olive oil, garlic and lemon juice.

3 Cut the basil leaves lengthways into thin strips and add them to the oil mixture.

4 Brush the slices of meat with the oil, season with salt and pepper and arrange them on 4 small individual plates.

5 Allow to marinate for at least 10 minutes and serve at room temperature.

LAMB FRITTERS

*Home-made Algerian dough, rolled, filled with
a lamb and herb stuffing and deep-fried.*

INGREDIENTS

PASTRY:

140 g/5 oz plain flour

2 tbsp olive oil

1 egg

1 tbsp water

FILLING:

280 g/10 oz leg of lamb

2 tbsp olive oil

½ onion, chopped

1 tbsp chopped coriander

Salt and pepper

1 egg, beaten

Oil for deep frying

SERVES: 4

TIME: Preparation takes about 45 minutes and cooking takes approximately 10 minutes, depending on how many batches are made.

1 To make the pastry, place the flour in a large bowl. Beat together the olive oil, egg and water and add to the flour. Work the mixture together to make a smooth dough and set aside.

2 Cut the meat into small cubes and fry in the 2 tbsp olive oil. Add the onion and coriander, and sauté another 2 minutes. Season with salt and pepper, then remove from the heat.

3 Reserve 1 tsp of the beaten egg and add the remainder to the meat. Beat all the ingredients together well.

4 Roll out the pastry very finely and cut small rounds out of it. Place a little of the stuffing on the centre of each round. Brush around the edge of each pastry with the reserved beaten egg. Fold into half moons and pinch the edges well to seal.

5 Heat the oil for deep frying and drop in a few of the half moons at a time. Remove with a slotted spoon when golden, drain on kitchen paper and serve hot.

Serving idea: Serve with a tossed salad and thin lemon slices.

Watchpoint: The edges of the pastries must be well sealed (or the stuffing will escape during cooking) – pinch firmly between thumb and forefinger.

Variation: Use different meat and herbs, such as veal or beef with parsley or fresh basil.

TURKISH LAMB

Stuffed lamb loin with a simple aubergine purée is perfect served as an elegant entrée.

INGREDIENTS

2 aubergines, peeled and diced

4 tbsp olive oil

Juice of 1 lemon

Salt and pepper

1 saddle of lamb, fatty parts removed

115 ml/4 fl oz lamb or chicken stock

SERVES: 4

TIME: Preparation takes about 45 minutes and cooking takes approximately 40 minutes.

Watchpoint: Roll the saddles up very delicately over the purée, trying not to push down too hard.

1 Fry the diced aubergines in half the olive oil. Pour over the lemon juice, cover and cook for 15 minutes shaking the pan from time to time. Season with salt and pepper.

2 When the aubergines are cooked, crush to a purée with a pestle and mortar. You will have to do this in batches.

3 Bone the saddle and separate it in two. Season one half of the saddle with salt and pepper, then spread over half of the purée, being careful not to go right up to the edges.

4 Carefully roll up the saddle, keeping the purée well inside. Truss the rolled meat with kitchen string sufficiently tightly to hold it together. Repeat with the other half of the saddle.

5 Lightly brown the two rolls in the remaining oil. Cook in a preheated 200°C/400°F/gas mark 6 oven for 20-30 minutes.

6 After removing from the oven, deglaze the pan with the stock, stirring well. Cut the rolls into slices and serve with the cooking juices.

LAMB AND MINT IN FILO PASTRY

A surprisingly simple and original lamb–filled pastry from the shores of North Africa.

INGREDIENTS

460 g/1 lb lamb (shoulder)

2 tbsp olive oil

1 onion, chopped

10 mint leaves, chopped

2 eggs

Salt

Chilli powder

Ras el hanout (ground cloves, cinnamon and black pepper, mixed)

3 tbsp butter

4 sheets filo pastry

A little beaten egg

SERVES: 4

TIME: Preparation takes about 30 minutes and cooking takes approximately 10 minutes.

1 Cut the meat into small pieces and gently fry in the oil. Do not allow it to brown. Add the onion and mint and fry for 1 minute.

2 Beat together the 2 eggs. Remove the pan with the meat from the heat and beat in the eggs. Keep beating until the mixture cools. Season with the salt, chilli powder and *ras el hanout* to taste.

3 Brush the butter over the separated sheets of pastry. Distribute the egg and meat mixture between the centre of the pastry pieces, then fold in the sides, working into a square shape. Seal the last fold of pastry with a little beaten egg.

4 Heat any remaining butter in a pan and fry the filo packets on both sides. Reduce the heat and continue to cook for another 5 minutes. Serve piping hot.

Checkpoint: Turn the filo pastries over frequently during the last 5 minutes of cooking so that they brown evenly.

Variation: The same type of stuffing could be made by substituting veal or beef and adding more or less herbs.

Cook's tip: Dried mint leaves keep their flavour for about 2 years. Dry separated leaves in a dry, warm place and then keep them in a well-sealed box.

*Above left: **Turkish Lamb**.*

Desserts and Cookies

A 'dessert' in the Mediterranean can mean anything from a piece of fruit to a deliciously sweet cookie. The climate in the region is just right for the cultivation of fruit, which is presented in various guises. Sweet pastries or sweetmeats may be presented later, as a between-meals snack. Strong coffee is served with these treats and the contrast between dainty sugary bites and the sapid bitterness exuded by the percolated beans is a memorable sensory experience.

Above: **Picking grapefruit in Galilee, Israel.**
Left: **The lush farmland of France married to the culinary inventiveness of its chefs produces a cuisine without parallel.**

ORANGE SORBET

INGREDIENTS

225 g/8 oz sugar
Zest of 1 orange
220 ml/8 fl oz fresh orange
   juice
75 ml/2½ fl oz fresh lemon
   juice

SERVES: 4-6

1 Dissolve the sugar in 440 ml/16 fl oz water, bring to the boil and boil for 10 minutes continuously. Set aside to cool.

2 Blanch the orange zest in boiling water. Mix the cooled syrup with the orange and lemon juice, and stir in the zest. Pour the mixture into a plastic container and place in the freezer.

3 Remove the sorbet from the freezer every 30 minutes and beat with a fork until it has completely crystallised.

TIME: Preparation takes about 10 minutes and freezing takes approximately 3-4 hours.

ZABAGLIONE WITH MARSALA

INGREDIENTS

8 egg yolks
115 g/4 oz sugar
2 tbsp almond Marsala
Pinch cinnamon

SERVES: 4

TIME: Preparation takes 5 minutes and cooking takes approximately 15 minutes.

1 Whisk the egg yolks with the sugar until the mixture is light and lemon coloured.

2 Add the Marsala and place the mixture in a double boiler or in a metal bowl over a saucepan of hot water. Beat until the zabaglione is thick enough to leave trails when dripped from a spoon.

3 Take the mixture off the heat and beat until cool. Pour into serving glasses and sprinkle with a little cinnamon before serving.

RHUBARB SORBET

INGREDIENTS
460 g/1 lb rhubarb
175 g/6 oz sugar
340 ml/12 fl oz water

SERVES: 4

TIME: Preparation takes about
10 minutes and freezing in an ice-
cream maker approximately 40 minutes.

1 Peel the rhubarb and cut the stalks
into small pieces.

2 Place the rhubarb in a saucepan with
the sugar and water. Bring to the boil
and cook for 5 minutes.

3 Blend the mixture with a hand mixer
until smooth and pour into the bowl of
an ice-cream maker.* Set the machine in
motion and remove when the sorbet is
crystallised. Spoon into a container and
keep in the freezer until needed.

* If an ice-cream maker is not available,
part freeze the mixture in a shallow
container, break up gently with a fork and
then pour into a covered container and
freeze until needed.

Left: **Orange and Rhubarb sorbets, served on a
bed of sliced fruit.**

ORANGE-FLAVOURED CREAM CARAMEL

In this recipe, traditional Algerian caramel custards are enhanced with the flavour of fresh orange peel.

INGREDIENTS

600 ml/1 pint milk

4 eggs

90-115 g/3-4 oz sugar

Zest of 1 orange, cut into thin slices

CARAMEL:

3 tbsp water

55 g/2 oz sugar

SERVES: 4

1 Bring the milk to a boil. Beat together the eggs and the sugar in a bowl. Pour the boiling milk over the egg mixture and stir continuously until thickened. Set aside to cool.

2 Boil the water and sugar together over high heat until a light caramel forms. Watch the mixture carefully so that the caramel does not darken too quickly.

3 Lightly grease 8 small ramekins. Pour a little caramel into the base of each ramekin, working quickly so that the caramel does not harden.

4 Blanch the orange zest in boiling water for 1 minute, drain and divide between the caramel-coated ramekins.

5 Skim off any mousse which has risen to the surface of the cream custard and fill each of the ramekins almost to the rim with the cooled custard.

6 Place the ramekins in a *bain-marie* in a preheated 140°C/275°F/gas mark 1 oven for approximately 30-40 minutes. Allow to cool then chill before serving.

Cook's tip: A *bain-marie* is a shallow ovenproof container half filled with hot water. Baking the ramekins in this manner prevents them overheating.

TIME: Preparation takes about 1 hour and cooking takes approximately 45 minutes. Chilling time is a few hours.

ALMOND SURPRISE BRICKS

*A flaky Moroccan dessert of ground almonds
rolled in filo pastry flavoured with honey.*

INGREDIENTS

225 g/8 oz ground almonds

4 tbsp sugar

Pinch cinnamon

175 ml/6 fl oz peanut oil

1 egg

8 sheets filo pastry

1 beaten egg

3 tbsp runny honey

SERVES: 4

TIME: Preparation takes about 40 minutes and cooking takes about 5 minutes.

1 Mix together the almonds and sugar. Sprinkle over cinnamon to taste.

2 Gently heat half the oil until just hot and add the almond mixture. Allow the mixture to brown lightly.

3 Meanwhile, beat the egg. Remove the almond mixture from the heat and briskly beat in the egg. Set aside to cool.

4 Fold each filo sheet into a long, narrow strip. Place the stuffing at the end and make a triangular packet by folding up one side over the stuffing, as if folding a flag. Brush the last fold with beaten egg to seal. Set aside.

5 Heat the remaining oil and fry the bricks for 1 minute on each side to brown slightly. Finish cooking in a preheated 200°C/400°F/gas mark 6 oven for approximately 3 minutes. Transfer to a serving dish.

6 Bring the honey to boil in a small saucepan and pour over the bricks.

Checkpoint: When you add the almond mixture to the oil, stir briskly and continuously as it tends to brown quickly.

FROMAGE FRAIS TARTS

These uniquely flavoured fresh cheese tarts are from the shores of the southern Mediterranean.

INGREDIENTS

PASTRY:

140 g/5 oz flour

Pinch salt

1½ tbsp sugar

½ beaten egg

4 tbsp butter, softened

FILLING:

2 eggs, separated

2 tbsp sugar

175 g/6 oz fromage frais

10 mint leaves, finely chopped

½ lemon peel, blanched and finely chopped

SERVES: 4

TIME: Preparation and resting take about 1 hour and cooking takes 20-30 minutes.

1 Place the flour in a bowl and add the salt, sugar and egg. Mixing with your fingers, add the butter and work into the flour and other ingredients.

2 Form the pastry into a ball and place in the refrigerator for 15 minutes.

3 When the pastry has rested, roll out on a floured surface and cut to fit 4 small, nonstick tart tins. Prick the bases and cook in a preheated 160°C/325°F/gas mark 3 oven for 10 minutes.

4 Meanwhile, make the filling. Beat together the egg yolks and sugar. Add the fromage frais, mint and lemon peel and mix well.

5 Whisk the egg whites to form stiff peaks, then carefully fold into the filling mixture. Fill the precooked tart cases and return to the oven for approximately 20 minutes. Serve hot or cold.

Serving idea: Thin a little fromage frais with milk, sweeten and pour over the tarts when served.

Cook's tip: This can be made as one large tart if you prefer.

Watchpoint: Do not overfill the tarts as the filling rises during cooking. Cover with foil should they begin to brown too quickly.

Variation: If fromage frais is not available, use sieved cottage cheese or ricotta thinned with a little milk.

ALMOND COOKIES

INGREDIENTS
115 g/4 oz ground almonds
105 g/3½ oz sugar
½ egg white
Few drops almond essence
2 tbsp pine nuts

SERVES: 4

TIME: Preparation takes about
10 minutes and cooking takes
approximately 30 minutes.

1 Mix together the almonds and sugar.
Add the egg white and 1-2 drops of
almond essence. Work well to form a
compact dough.

2 Shape the dough into small rounds
and place them on a floured baking
sheet, spacing them well apart to allow
the cookies to spread. Sprinkle with the
pine nuts.

3 Bake in a preheated 160°C/325°F/
gas mark 3 oven for 30-40 minutes.

CITRUS FRUIT SALAD WITH ORANGE-FLOWER WATER

A simple and refreshing fruit salad from Israel.

INGREDIENTS
4 yellow grapefruit
4 oranges
2 limes
2 tsp orange-flower water
10 basil leaves
2 tbsp sugar

SERVES: 4

TIME: Preparation takes about 30 minutes and marinating takes at least 6 hours.

Cook's tip: If orange-flower water is unavailable, it can be replaced with an orange-flavoured liqueur.

Left: **Citrus Fruit Salad with Orange-flower Water.**
Above right: **Succulent grapefruit ripen in the sun at Galilee, Israel.**

1 Peel the fruit and then carefully remove the flesh segments, reserving any juice. Place the fruit segments decoratively on a serving plate.

2 Add the juice to the orange-flower water.

3 Cut the basil leaves into very thin strips and sprinkle over the fruit, along with the sugar. Pour over the juice and orange-flower water.

4 Leave to marinate in the refrigerator for approximately 6 hours.

SPANISH CREAM FLANS

INGREDIENTS

600 ml/1 pint milk

175 ml/6 fl oz single cream

4 eggs

115 g/4 oz icing sugar

Few pinches cinnamon

1 tbsp demerara sugar

SERVES: 4

TIME: Preparation takes about 15 minutes and cooking takes approximately 35 minutes.

1 Mix together the milk and cream.

2 In another bowl, beat together the eggs and icing sugar.

3 Stir the milk mixture into the eggs and sugar, adding cinnamon to taste.

4 Pour the mixture into 8 small ramekins and cook in a preheated 150°C/300°F/gas mark 2 oven for approximately 35 minutes – the flans should be quite solid when cooked.

5 Sprinkle a little sugar over each flan and place under a hot grill for 1 minute to caramelise. Serve warm or cold.

PEACH SHERBET

INGREDIENTS

460 g/1 lb fresh ripe peaches

175 g/6 oz sugar

Juice of 1 lemon

SERVES: 4

TIME: Preparation takes about 40 minutes plus freezing.

1 Peel the peaches and remove the stones. Chop the flesh.

2 Place the peaches in the bowl of an electric mixer with the lemon juice and sugar. Mix until the sugar dissolves.

3 Pour the peach mixture into an ice-cream maker and process according to manufacturer's directions. The ice cream should be allowed to remain frozen for a few hours. Serve the sherbet with segments of fresh peach.

Right: Peach Sherbet from Italy is made with only the simplest of ingredients: fresh ripe peaches, sugar and the juice of a lemon.

CHURROS

INGREDIENTS

120 ml/4 fl oz milk
120 ml/4 fl oz water
Salt
140 g/5 oz flour
2 egg yolks
Oil for deep frying
Sugar
Cinnamon

SERVES: 4

TIME: Preparation takes 25 minutes and cooking takes about 30 minutes.

1 Bring the milk and water to the boil with a pinch of salt. Sieve the flour in gradually so that no lumps form. Stir the mixture well.

2 Allow the mixture to cool slightly and beat in the egg yolks. Heat the oil to 170°C/335°F.

3 Place the churros mixture in a piping bag with a wide straight nozzle. Squeeze out long ribbons, or 'churros', into the oil and cut off from the nozzle with a knife.

4 Allow the churros to brown lightly; remove and drain on kitchen paper. Serve sprinkled with sugar and cinnamon.

SEMOLINA CAKE

INGREDIENTS
600 ml/1 pint milk
1 tsp orange-flower water
3 tbsp sugar
2 tbsp raisins
55 g/2 oz semolina
2 egg yolks (optional)

SERVES: 4

TIME: Preparation takes
15 minutes, cooking takes
5 minutes and setting
takes at least 2 hours.

1 Place the milk, orange-flower water, sugar and raisins in a saucepan, stir and bring to the boil.

2 Reduce the heat and add the semolina, stirring continuously. Mix in the egg yolks, if using. Stir until the mixture thickens – about 5 minutes.

3 Pour the mixture into a large serving dish or individual dishes and refrigerate for at least 2 hours to set.

4 Turn out of the dish, if desired, before serving.

Serving idea: A fresh fruit coulis (crushed fruit, diluted with a little water and sweetened with sugar) makes a good topping.

Watchpoint: Stir the mixture continuously, otherwise it will become lumpy and will stick and scorch.

*Right: **Semolina Cake from Egypt may be enjoyed as a dessert, or as a snack with coffee.***

PEAR SORBET

INGREDIENTS
460 g/1 lb pears, peeled and
    chopped
5 tbsp sugar
3 tbsp lemon juice
1 egg white and a pinch of
    salt, whipped until stiff

SERVES: 4-6

1 Dissolve the sugar in 150 ml/5 fl oz water, add the chopped pear, bring to the boil and boil continuously for 10 minutes. Set aside to cool.

2 Once cool, blend the pear pulp in a blender until smooth. Stir in the lemon juice, pour into a plastic container and freeze for 1 hour.

3 After 1 hour, remove the sorbet and beat it well with a fork. Incorporate the beaten egg white gently, using a metal spoon.

4 Cover and return to the freezer until required.

TIME: Preparation takes about 30 minutes and freezing takes about 2 hours.

LEBANESE BUTTER BISCUITS

These delicate biscuits are simple to make and always popular.

INGREDIENTS

175 g/6 oz butter, softened

225 g/8 oz sugar

225 g/8 oz flour

A few drops almond essence

Butter for greasing

1 tbsp flaked hazelnuts

1 tbsp flaked almonds

SERVES: 4

TIME: Preparation takes about 15 minutes and cooking takes approximately 20 minutes.

Checkpoint: The biscuit dough is very fragile and cannot be rolled. Spread a little dough out with your fingers and cut it with a pastry cutter, if desired.

Variation: Replace the hazelnuts and almonds with crushed walnuts.

1 Beat the softened butter for 3 minutes. Add the sugar and beat until the sugar has dissolved.

2 Add the flour and mix the dough with your fingers. Add the almond essence and work the dough once again. Break the dough into pieces and shape into rough circles with your hands.

3 Grease a baking sheet with the butter and place the cookies on the sheet. Sprinkle with nuts.

4 Bake in a preheated 180°C/350°F/gas mark 4 oven for 20-30 minutes, checking from time to time.

GNOCCHI WITH PRUNE FILLING

Sweet gnocchi dough is rolled around a prune that has been flavoured with sugar and cinnamon.

INGREDIENTS

24 prunes, stoned

450 g/1 lb potatoes, steamed in their skins

125 g/4 oz flour

½ egg, beaten

15 ml/1 tbsp milk

50 g/2 oz butter

Sugar

Cinnamon

45 ml/3 tbsp Eau de Vie (fruit flavoured alcohol)

SERVES: 4

TIME: Preparation takes about 30 minutes and cooking takes approximately 30 minutes.

1 Peel the steamed potatoes and dry them on kitchen paper. Push the potatoes through a fine sieve.

2 Beat the egg, milk and 25 g/1 oz butter into the potatoes. Mix really well and then add the flour, beating constantly.

3 When the mixture is really well mixed, form the dough into a ball.

4 Sprinkle a little sugar and cinnamon into each of the stoned prunes.

5 With floured fingers, break off a little gnocchi dough and wrap this around the prune, making sure that the dough is well sealed around the prunes.

6 Bring a large saucepan of water to boiling, add the gnocchi and cook them until they rise to the surface. Remove with a slotted spoon and set aside to dry on a cloth.

7 Heat the remaining butter in a frying pan and sauté the gnocchi, sprinkling

over more sugar and cinnamon to taste. Pour over a little Eau de Vie and serve.

Checkpoint: Avoid making the gnocchi covering too thick. Serve warm.

Variation: Fresh plums can be substitued for the prunes. Sprinkle over thin strips of mint to decorate.

POACHED PEARS IN PORT

A French dish to serve either hot or cold. The pears retain the flavour of the port and are absolutely delicious.

INGREDIENTS
4 large pears, peeled
Juice of 1 lemon
600 ml/1 pint port
1 tsp cinnamon
250 g/9 oz sugar

SERVES: 4

1 Pour the lemon juice over the peeled pears to prevent them discolouring.

2 Place the pears in a large saucepan, add the port and just enough water to cover. Sprinkle over the cinnamon and the sugar. Cook on a gentle heat until the pears soften – test with the point of a knife.

3 Remove the pears and either keep warm or chill in the refrigerator.

4 Put the juice back on a brisk heat and allow to reduce and become slightly syrupy. Pour the sauce over the pears and serve.

Serving idea: Instead of serving the pears whole, the flesh can be shaped into balls using a melon baller.

Watchpoint: Watch the juice carefully in step 4 as it tends to reduce quite quickly and will thicken too much if not removed from the heat rapidly.

TIME: Preparation takes about 5 minutes and cooking takes approximately 1 hour and 20 minutes.

Right: **Poached Pears in Port.**
Left: **The harbour at St. Tropez, a famous holiday resort on France's Côte d'Azur.**

WALNUT MONTECAOS

INGREDIENTS

55 g/2 oz sugar

140 g/5 oz flour

55-90 g/2-3 oz finely ground walnuts

115 ml/4 fl oz oil

1 tsp crushed walnuts

SERVES: 4

TIME: Preparation takes 20 minutes and cooking takes 20 minutes.

1 In a large bowl, mix together the sugar and flour. Add the ground walnuts and mix well.

2 Add the oil little by little, mixing with your fingers. Now add the crushed walnuts and mix everything together well into a dough.

3 Break the dough into small balls and place them on a floured baking sheet. Bake in a preheated 200°C/400°F/gas mark 6 oven for 5 minutes, then reduce the heat to 150°C/300°F/gas mark 2 and bake for another 15 minutes.

GYPSY'S ARM

This intriguing sounding recipe is a Spanish version of cream-filled sponge roll.

INGREDIENTS

SPONGE CAKE:

4 eggs, beaten

100 g/3¼ oz sugar

105 g/3½ oz flour

Salt

CRÈME PATISSIÈRE:

2 egg yolks

75 g/2½ oz sugar

1 tbsp cornflour

1 tbsp flour

300 ml/½ pint boiling milk

Pinch cinnamon

Peel of 1 orange, blanched
and finely chopped

SERVES: 4

TIME: Preparation takes about 35 minutes, cooking takes approximately 20 minutes and chilling takes about 2 hours.

1 To make the sponge cake, beat together the 4 eggs, sugar, flour and a pinch of salt.

2 Grease a large rectangle of greaseproof paper with butter and place it in a long, wide rectangular baking sheet. Cut the paper to fit exactly onto the baking sheet.

3 Pour the sponge mixture onto the baking sheet and bake in a preheated 200°C/400°F/gas mark 6 oven for 15-20 minutes. The sponge should not brown, but test it is done. Cool slightly.

4 While the sponge is cooking, make the filling. Beat together the egg yolks, sugar, cornflour and flour in a saucepan. Add boiling milk gradually, stirring constantly. Continue stirring over a low heat until the mixture thickens. Remove from the heat and add the cinnamon and orange zest. Cool.

5 Cover the slightly warm sponge cake in the baking tray with a slightly damp tea towel.

6 Turn the sponge out onto the tea towel, peel off the greaseproof paper and roll up the sponge tightly in the tea towel. Leave to cool for 30 minutes.

7 Once cool, unroll and spread the cream evenly over the inside. Re-roll in the tea towel and chill in the refrigerator for approximately 2 hours. Cut into slices to serve.

Serving idea: Flavour the crème patissière with orange liqueur and accompany it with fresh peach segments.

Checkpoint: The rolling-up of the sponge should be done as quickly as possible. The sponge should also be rolled as tightly as possible.

Cook's tip: The sponge should be very thin, so that it is easy to roll up.

PROFITEROLES WITH CHOCOLATE SAUCE

A great French classic — light choux pastry cases filled with vanilla ice cream and coated with hot chocolate sauce.

INGREDIENTS

CHOUX PASTRY:

220 ml/8 fl oz water

90 g/3 oz butter

Pinch salt

150 g/6 oz plain flour, sieved

5 large eggs, beaten

CHOCOLATE SAUCE:

150 g/6 oz dark chocolate, melted

2 tbsp sugar

100 ml/4 fl oz whipping cream

FILLING:

600 ml/1 pint vanilla ice cream

SERVES: 6

TIME: Preparation takes about 25 minutes and cooking takes 1 hour.

1 Bring the water to the boil in a saucepan and add the butter and salt. Remove from the heat as soon as the butter has melted and beat in the flour, a little at a time. Allow to dry out.

2 Reserve a little of the beaten egg for brushing and beat the rest into the flour mixture. Fill a piping bag fitted with a plain tip with the mixture.

3 Grease 2 baking sheets and pipe 12 small balls of choux pastry on to them, spreading the balls well apart. Mix the remaining beaten egg with a little water and brush over the choux pastry balls.

4 Bake the balls in a preheated 220°C/425°F/gas mark 7 oven for 10 minutes, then reduce the heat to 180°C/350°F/ gas mark 4 and cook for approximately 20 minutes more – the balls should double in size and be golden brown.

5 Remove from the oven and pierce them to let the steam escape. Turn off the oven, leave the door open, and put

the profiteroles back in the open oven to dry out for about 10 minutes.

6 Melt the chocolate and the sugar together over a pan of boiling water, then stir in the cream.

7 Slice open the pastry cases, fill with ice cream and pour over the chocolate sauce.

TARTE TATIN

A lightly caramelised apple tart that is cooked with the crust uppermost and then turned over on serving.

INGREDIENTS
460 g/1 lb flaky pastry
1 kg/2¼ lb apples, peeled,
   halved and cored
90 g/3 oz butter
175 g/6 oz sugar
3 tbsp double cream

1 Dot the base of a pie tin with the butter and sprinkle over half the sugar.

2 Place the apple halves, rounded side down, onto the butter and sugar, and sprinkle over the remaining sugar.

3 Roll the pastry out into a round just slightly larger than the bottom of the tin.

4 Place the pastry round over the apples, tucking it down at the edges, and cook in a preheated 230°C/450°F/gas mark 8 oven for approximately 30 minutes.

5 Remove from the oven when cooked and turn immediately onto a serving plate.

6 Whip the cream and serve in a small bowl for the guests to help themselves.

Serving idea: The tart can be served either hot or cold.

Cook's tip: Tuck the pastry down well at the edges, so that when you turn the cooked tart over onto the serving plate all the caramel is trapped on top of the tart.

SERVES: 6

TIME: Preparation takes 15 minutes and cooking takes 30 minutes.

FRUIT SALAD

INGREDIENTS

115 g/4 oz redcurrants

115 g/4 oz blackcurrants

175 g/6 oz strawberries

115 g/4 oz blackberries

115 g/4 oz raspberries

115 g/4 oz red gooseberries

115 g/4 oz green gooseberries

115 g/4 oz wild strawberries

115 g/4 oz cassis berries

115 g/4 oz blueberries

Juice of 2 oranges

55 g/2 oz sugar

1 tsp fruit alcohol (orange, peach or cherry liqueur or eau de vie)

SERVES: 4

TIME: Preparation takes 30 minutes and 2 hours for marinating.

1 Wash, trim and chop the fruit as necessary.

2 Place the fruit in a large bowl and add the orange juice, sugar and fruit alcohol.

3 Place in the refrigerator for 2 hours, turning the ingredients from time to time.

APPLES WITH PINE NUTS AND HONEY

This Libyan dish is always popular. Apples are sautéed in butter and honey, and served with raisins and pine nuts.

INGREDIENTS
4 Golden Delicious apples
Juice of 1 lemon
2 tbsp butter
3 tbsp pine nuts
1 tbsp raisins
2 tbsp honey
1 tbsp orange-flower water

1 Peel and core the apples. Cut each apple into quarters and sprinkle with lemon juice to keep from browning.

2 Heat the butter and sauté the apple pieces over a moderate heat.

3 Add the pine nuts and raisins, cook for 1 minute, then add the honey.

4 Turn the apples quickly in the pan so that they caramelise evenly. Deglaze with the orange-flower water. Serve hot.

Buying guide: Any variety of firm apple can be used in this recipe.

Cook's tip: At step 4, turn the apples rapidly and frequently so they are coated and coloured evenly.

Checkpoint: When you add the honey to the pan it will come to the boil quickly. You must turn the apple pieces immediately, and caramelise them sufficiently, before deglazing with the orange-flower water.

SERVES: 4

TIME: **Preparation takes about 30 minutes and cooking takes approximately 10 minutes.**

APPLE FRITTERS

INGREDIENTS

115 g/4 oz apples, peeled, cored
   and cut into small pieces
115 ml/4 fl oz orange juice
55 ml/2 fl oz Marsala
225 g/8 oz flour, sieved
1.25 ml/¼ tsp baking powder
30 g/1 oz ground almonds
55 g/2 oz sugar
2 egg yolks
115 ml/4 fl oz milk
Oil for deep frying

SERVES: 4

1 Marinate the apple in the orange juice and the Marsala for 15 minutes.

2 Mix together the flour, baking powder and the ground almonds.

3 Whisk together the sugar and egg yolks until quite white. Add the flour mixture, beating in well. Stir in the milk and beat thoroughly.

4 Add the flour and egg mixture to the apples in their marinade. Stir gently to blend the ingredients together evenly. Allow to rest for 10 minutes.

5 Heat the oil in a deep pan and gently add spoonfuls of apple and fritter mixture. Allow to cook through and turn golden brown, then remove with a slotted spoon.

6 Drain on kitchen paper and serve either hot or cold.

TIME: Preparation takes about 15 minutes and cooking takes about 20 minutes.

Right: **Apple Fritters from Italy.**

ALMOND-FILLED COOKIES

These rich Egyptian tea cookies are filled with ground almonds.

INGREDIENTS

PASTRY:

100 g/3¼ oz butter, softened

140 g/5 oz flour

2 tsp orange-flower water

30 g/1 oz dates, chopped

FILLING:

115 g/4 oz ground almonds

90 g/3 oz icing sugar

1 tsp water

TO SERVE:

2 tbsp sugar

Pinch cinnamon

SERVES: 4

TIME: Preparation and resting time for the pastry is about 1 hour. Cooking takes approximately 20 minutes.

1 Rub the butter into the flour, add the orange-flower water and dates, and work the pastry into a neat ball. Set aside to rest in the refrigerator for 15 minutes.

2 Place the almonds, icing sugar and water in a blender and mix until a firm paste is obtained.

3 Pull off small pieces of the pastry dough and shape into small balls. Make an indentation on top with your thumb large enough to hold a little filling.

4 Place a little of the filling in the centre and fold up the edges, sealing in the filling, to form small balls.

5 Place the cookies on a greased baking tray and cook in a preheated 200°C/400°F/gas mark 6 oven for 20 minutes. Allow to cool and then sprinkle with sugar and cinnamon.

INDEX